The Four People You Marry

Bill and Traci Vanderbush

Sometimes the purest of hearts are birthed in the darkest places. This is one of the mysteries of grace. This is the mysterious way of love.
~ Traci Vanderbush

Contents

Introduction

"Love."

All have desired it. Some have tasted, touched and seen glimpses of authentic love while wading through the mire of love's counterfeits. Part of love's mystery is the way it makes itself known in the midst of hatred, confusion, and all kinds of darkness. Often, we learn what love is by experiencing what love is not. Many have experienced the outer core of love, but how much of humanity will be able to touch the core of love and be immersed in its fullness?

Being immersed in the fullness of love requires vulnerability, nakedness of the heart and soul, and a life without secrets. I once heard someone say, "You are only as sick as your secrets." And they were right. "Therefore, confess your trespasses to one another, and pray for one another, that you may be healed. The effective, fervent prayer of a righteous man avails much." ~James 5:16 NKJV

Confession to a heart of authentic love brings healing, because the hearer fervently prays for the freedom of one tormented by secrets, and the authentic lover will never treat one according to what they have done wrong, but according to their true identity as a whole person. Once a person has stripped their heart bare, their eyes become opened to see themselves clearly in the mirror, and they are empowered to live a life of wholeness. This is what love does.

The vulnerability and revealing of ourselves that brings the face of love into our vision and takes us into the heart of love, is a risky, sometimes painful journey. But if one pushes past fear and embraces even the difficult parts of the quest, there will be no room for disappointment. Each of our journeys is different. I have come to believe that no ones' journey is easy. Along the pathway created by our choices and the choices of others, ultimately we will come to know that love is not a feeling or philosophy, but Love is a person. And He has been with us all along.

> *Often, we learn what love is by experiencing what love is not.*

In the following pages, each thought is simply a part of the unfolding revelation from our own, personal experiences. We have come to believe that there is a depth to love that man can only hope to know while alive on this earth, and we long to fall deeper into it. We invite you into our thought processes and we pray you will find yourself falling in love with your partner all over again. It is possible!

~ Traci Vanderbush

Chapter 1

The Crucible of Transformation

"God has sovereignly designed a world in which we get to experience the power of personal responsibility."
Bill

"Marriage is the great crucible of transformation where you both agree, before God and man, to kill each other." When my dear friend, Ted, said this to me one day, I responded with dismissive laughter as we lounged on the porch soaking up the vista of the Texas hill country. But inside, I knew that on some deeply profound level, this was true. Marriage is a journey of metamorphosis. You have come here to let go, together, to lay your life down. If we could see into the motives beneath the usual wedding vows, and could bring that to the surface, they would probably read something like this. *"I take you into my life, to overpower you, and to change you to be more like me. All along I'll do my best to please you without giving up anything that would bring me pleasure as well. With everything in my power, I will do my best to eliminate your faults, and to turn you into the perfect person who will never disappoint me and will live to bring me joy. And you can have some too, if you cooperate. Together we will build the dream I've always wanted."* In some twisted way, we make our spouse into an idol, shaping them into an object worthy of our worship, assuring that they bring us happiness. I think we can all agree, if there's any hint of selfishness in us, it hasn't done us any good. Simply stated, God is committed to bringing us to an awareness that, in Him, we are already complete, and this will bring us to the end of ourselves. And so begins the transformation, not only of our spouse, but of self, and us together.

Everywhere I look, people are searching for love. And to find the best quality of love, we have somehow concluded that we must find the "one." Of the billions of humans walking this planet, we can thin the herd out to the eligible. For example, if you're a woman looking for a man, half of the population is already off the table. Take the remainder and eliminate the married ones and those under and over your target age range. Keep those with the general look that you're after, those who have a decent job, then figure that from that pool of people, you probably want one that likes cats and kids, and there are about four guys left. Okay, I'm kidding, and that's not what the title of this book is about. But when it comes to love, most people are looking for the one person who has it all. You may find someone who seems to be the one, but the journey from, "Do you come here often?" to " Can you grab the diaper bag?" can make you feel like you're going crazy. That is unless you come to a valuable relationship revelation that most will discover, given enough time, even if they don't have language to put to it. So here, in a nutshell, is what we're about to unpack. There are four people in that "one" that you got into a relationship with. They are:

1. *The person you think they are.*
2. *The person they think they are.*
3. *The person they are right now.*
4. *The person they are becoming.*

Problems arise when you only fall in love with one or two out of the four. When one of the others shows up that you didn't plan on, you can feel like you got fooled into marrying someone who wasn't who you thought they were. The day this happens is the day you wake up, look over to the other side of the bed and wonder, "Who are you and what have I done?"

"I didn't sign up for this."

Have you ever said or thought that? Then this book is for you. I'm going to do a boldly presumptive thing throughout this book that may offend you, and I'm okay with that. I'm not going to tell you what to think, but I am going to write as if I know what you think. I understand that may be offensive, since everyone thinks differently. But as you read this, it may strike you with some measure of surprise as over and over again, it seems like I was writing this just for you or with you in mind. When that happens, just know this. You're not alone. Every thought that Traci and I project in this book is common feedback from years of conversations and listening. Whether you're in a great marriage or a difficult marriage, anytime you feel out of control, it's lonely. But take heart, for you most certainly are not alone.

By the title of this book, you might think that the only possible way this could apply to your situation is if you married a schizophrenic. But then again, if you're reading this, you just might be desperate enough to wonder if they are, or maybe if you are. Many of us never really know the person we married before the moment we said "I do." We just happened to find something in this person that caused us to begin to consider a future with them and become uncomfortable with the thought of a life without them. Let me reassure you, you're not crazy and neither is your spouse (unless they are, and then that's another book altogether). I'm not talking about deliberate deception either. None of us know who we really are, but we have some ideas. And those ideas are formed by a number of factors. When we were born into this world, we had no idea how to be, what to like or dislike, what to believe, or how to behave. We have just one thing, and it's a lot of that one thing; we have other people. So we grow up watching the people around us and it is from them that we learn the most. When we watch someone enjoy something, we want that something too.

Rene Girard popularized this fact in psychology and called it the "theory of mimetic contagion." In other words, we mimic someone else and what we learn from one person becomes contagious to another who is watching us in the same way that we watched our influencer. Many studies have been done on the effect we have on each other in this way. For example, if you take two children who don't even know each other, and give them the same exact toy in the same exact package, something fascinating happens. After an initial fixation on their new possession, they begin to compare themselves and their toy to the same toy the other child has. Inevitably, one child will enjoy the toy more than the other. The child who enjoys the toy less will put their toy down and do something remarkable. They will try to take the toy from the other child.

Ultimately, it's not the toy they want. It's the joy.

The frustration comes from the notion that for some reason, the other child is having more fun than we are, so therefore what they have must be better. The realization that came from these studies is that we as humans watch what other people enjoy in order to discover what we should like or prefer. Another way to put it is,

10

that we don't know how to be human without each other. So in this quest to learn to be ourselves, we are created to be attracted to each other. Yet, opposites attract because we are intrigued by the differences of another, wondering subconsciously if the way they are may be better than the way we are.

Different isn't good or bad. It's just different. If you assume that different is bad, then everyone different than you is worse, and that can make you tough to get along with. If you assume that different is good, then you may spend your entire life trying to be someone else. Neither of these things helps you in discovering your true identity. So let the idea of good and bad go, and simply embrace "different" and rename it "diversity" in your mind. This will keep you from turning your spouse into an enemy when the diversity gets annoying.

The very thing in your spouse that you find the most attractive may be the thing that also drives you mad. In seeking out an opposite, we're just naturally expanding our own boundaries of our own perception of ourselves. And so, in searching for yourself, you may fall in love with someone else who is often nothing at all like you.

THE MYSTERY OF LIMERENCE

Some words are so profound, that in their repetition, they become trite cliches easily dismissed. Nat King Cole sang a profound truth in the song "Nature Boy," when he said, "The greatest thing you'll ever learn, is just to love and be loved in return." When you feel loved by someone, and feel love for someone, a chemical cocktail triggers in your mind that has come to be known among psychologists as "limerence." You might know it as infatuation, but don't dismiss it, because it can be as deep and intense as any

11

emotion you can experience. Because it feels so intense, it can seem eternal, as if nothing could ever change the way you feel in this euphoric bliss. In the moment, it seems like it will last forever. But that's the danger of limerence. Eventually, the effect dissipates and leaves you with only the faint and fading memories of the way things felt. People addicted to the "feeling" of falling in love, are substituting the reality of long term love for the temporal, adrenaline-soaked high of the falling. Here's what it's like:

Limerence isolates your focus like a laser and if life can be seen as a play, you and the other person become the leads in a world of supporting roles, crazy adventure, deep melodrama, and reckless affection. The bottom line to all of this is that you are experiencing extreme selfishness, disguised as an isolated couple who "fell in love." The two of you are all important and alone in a world that just doesn't understand that you're having an experience that's so deeply spiritual, that surely, nobody else has ever experienced it before. Right here, let me just say that this is also how affairs happen. Even after marriage, even when there are no problems, and the relationship has taken on the comfort of a familiar easy chair, someone's well timed words or intriguing personality can trigger a limerence in you. If you allow that to continue without putting an intentional stop to it, you can selfishly sabotage your current relationship through an emotional or physical affair and cause tremendous pain. Limerence creates that deep heart connection between people that makes it maddeningly easy for good people to justify selfish actions and call it love. If you're presently in this situation, I understand that you can say the love is real, and I agree it is. But it's been twisted into a place where lying and betrayal are justified byproducts of what could have been an affection as caring and pure as heaven itself. "Love one another" is the command of Christ, and the moment we betray others in our expression of that command, we have lost the plot.

True Love is a person named Jesus Christ, and there is grace for you if any of this describes your past or present story. It is my prayer that through the understanding you receive from the insight of this book, that the pain of the past is healed, the confusion of the present is clarified, and the uncertainty of the future is replaced with hope. Unfaithfulness doesn't have to haunt your past, define your present, or become a part of your future story.

GROWING APART AND GROWING TOGETHER

I would theorize that every three to five years, you will be able to look back and see some significant changes from how you were just a few years ago. You think far differently from age ten to age fifteen. The changes are just as dramatic from age fifteen to age twenty. Now if you got married young (Traci and I met at age five and married when I was eighteen and she was nineteen), and you are now in your forties, you have, in essence, been married to a person who has undergone

> *Passive neglect is how things break down.*

substantial changes. They think differently, they look differently, and they may hardly resemble the person you married. Young couples are especially at risk for marriage problems if they don't understand and give grace for these changes. If you aren't prepared for these changes in yourself and your spouse, you may find yourselves growing apart. If you know this is the case, and keep open and honest communication about moments of learning and understanding, then you can guide that growth process to a place of growing together.

Growing is inevitable. How you grow is intentional. Purposeful actions that create quality, lasting memories will cultivate that growth as a union. Passive neglect is how things break down. God has sovereignly designed a world in which we get to experience the power of personal responsibility. You have the power to cultivate or neglect life, love, sin, addiction, worship, intimacy, spirituality, health, and mind. Whatever you cultivate will grow and flourish and what you choose to neglect will eventually lose its life. While it is my hope that this book saves marriages, restores lives, empowers hope, protects children, promotes intimacy, and preserves covenant, I have one desire above all of that. I want you to discover who you truly are. Because it all begins there.

Chapter 2

The Myth in Your Mind

"'I choose you,' may be the most powerful three words in the English language."
Bill

The first person you marry is the person you think they are.

This is the person you created in your mind the first time you felt attracted to your spouse, and you carried that image all through the relational dance that led you to say "yes." Dating life is a sales pitch for a time share. You don't get to know the hidden maintenance fees up front. All you know is the perfect, idealistic vision before your eyes. When speaking to others about your spouse, this is the person that you describe when your spouse isn't around. The person you think they are exists in some form. How you describe them to others is determined by two factors:

1. How you feel about them right now
2. How badly you want to impress the person you're talking with

That second factor is especially powerful, because when you're talking to someone whom you wish to impress in regards to your spouse, it reveals who you want your spouse to be, down in the depth of your soul and in the deepest neural pathways of your mind. The problem is that we create a character that they can never live up to. It's nearly impossible to live up to the expectation of a person who, in their imagination, is always trying to change you into who they have already decided you are. Only God gets that level of creative license.

And let's be real. Our culture of beautiful storytelling has beautified the story to the point where reality can't possibly measure up consistently. Remember every romantic comedy you've ever seen, where for the entire movie, neither character goes to the bathroom, smells like a dead fish, or looks disheveled. When the couple eventually hooks up, the implied sex is symphonic, choreographed perfection. There are no blemishes, no cellulite dimples, and the ideal soundtrack is always playing. In the perfect sunlit morning they wake, facing each other, and kiss. Every couple knows that after eight hours of sleep, you're more likely to hear, "Turn the other way. Your breath is bleaching my hair."

PLAYING THE HITS

Let's go back to the beginning. The surprising and voyeuristic reality of the first impression created the opening scene in an increasingly complex play in which each of you believes you are the director. Attraction enters the picture and because neither of you wants it to go wrong, both of you take control. The person you portray is the best of you, and these moments become your greatest hits. You know what happens to a band when it has a hit? It has to play that hit over and over again or else the audience simply won't be happy. If what you put on display is an appealing, but inauthentic representation of who you are, you may be stuck with having to replay that "hit" over and over until you just can't take it anymore.

I know it would be easiest to just be honest, but let's be honest about honesty. You honestly don't want to say the wrong thing, act the wrong way, or come across as misrepresenting the character you've created. You vacuum a normally dirty car, wear normally neglected cologne, or you put extra touches of aesthetic embellishments on your face and hair. This is dating, and it's a dance created to impress, by putting on display who you could be if you cared enough to be your best self. And because of the other person, suddenly you do care. This adds to the appeal of the relationship because now they are bringing out the best in you or making you a better person. The relationship will lack depth until the facade breaks down enough for them to experience hurt or disappointment.

This is important to the relationship because it's one thing to know you're loved, but it's another thing entirely to know that you're accepted. The most powerful words you ever hear may not be "I love you," but instead they might be, "I choose you." It is when you know that you're chosen, that you feel free to be at rest in being loved. This is also the core of our rest in being loved by God. When we realize that He believes in us and has chosen us, then we are able to believe in and experience His love.

The person you believe your spouse is, is the one you choose and the one you fall in love with. But that's not the version that remains, and it is not the only version of them that will show up over the course of time. Knowing this will prepare your heart to walk out the journey of the relationship to its most beautiful conclusion. Understanding the plot twist that's coming will make

17

all the difference in whether yours is a romance, drama, comedy, tragedy, satire, documentary, fiction, nonfiction, mystery, or horror story. Give the story enough time, and you might find that it's all of those, often at the same time.

So give yourself permission to predict and project what you have predetermined them to be on the basis of your personal priorities. There's nothing wrong with sitting down to watch the Super Bowl with an ideal outcome in your mind that you're hoping the game will live up to, except that marriage is not a game, and you are not merely an observer. But there are similarities. The joy, the pain, the euphoria, the sweat, the struggle, and the payoff, all of this is real. Life will force you to let go of your prediction. And perhaps the hardest lesson in marriage is just that. Letting go.

> *The most powerful words you ever hear may not be "I love you," but instead they might be, "I choose you."*

Mastering the Art of Letting Go

Classic Christian musician, Keith Green, sold and gave away truckloads of copies of his album, "No Compromise." No wonder. Think about that phrase. Do you feel that? You know, the primal *fist-in-the-air* superiority that makes you feel like purging your life of, well, pretty much everything? That phrase has been an anthem of Christian ideology that incites stadiums filled with people to move to an altar and lay down their lives for the Gospel. When it comes to following the call of God on your life, it's beautiful. But if you carry that same ideology of "no compromise" into every area of your marriage, it will kill the formation of understanding.

Marriage includes two wills entangled with one another, and for it to work, there must be compromise. Sorry, Keith, and every pastor ever. Marriage is like salvation. It doesn't work without surrender. Letting go means giving in without giving up. It is courageously trusting in something outside of yourself. Letting go is giving yourself a chance to be surprised, to be loved, even to be hurt. Letting go is not an act of weakness, in that something has overpowered you. Letting go is an act of strength. It's a confidence in your ability to adapt and thrive in any circumstance.

Picture a person with a parachute leaping from a plane into the darkness. A relative of mine, who was an Airborne Ranger, said that the most terrifying, exhilarating, and memorable jumps he ever did in combat were in the darkness in enemy territory. You let everything go to your training, your equipment, your team, and your task, and you leap into the night. You can't predict the outcome, but you know what you have to do. Standing at the altar, vowing to be one together forever is leaping into the night. If marriage isn't terrifying, exhilarating, and memorable, you're doing it wrong.

> *Letting go is an act of strength.*

But letting go also means letting go of the need to maintain the terrifying exhilaration all the time. On some days, it's healthy to let go of the need to make everything a defining moment. Fleming and John, an alternative husband-and-wife band that never made it big but should have, wrote a song many years ago called, "Comfortable." Apparently they had achieved a modicum of letting go in their musical marriage, and they decided to write a song about it.

"You know how to hold my hand,
You know how to make me mad,
You know everything about me.
We've been together longer,
Than most of our friends have,
But they don't know that it's not always a party.

Sometimes I try to shake it up,
Tickle the passion, wake it up.
It's time to breathe a little fire,
But you just put your arms around me,
And I let go of all my anxiety,
You know you're my lazy boy recliner.

I gotta tell you how I'm feeling,
In case you haven't noticed,
The mystery is gone.
Infatuation's wearing off.
I gotta tell you how I'm feeling,
I think that you'll agree,
That we've become predictable,
But I really don't mind being this comfortable."

It's that last line, *but I really don't mind being this comfortable*, that gets me. If you've ever watched people who've been together for decades and yet they're still devoted to doing life as one, they've mastered the art of letting go. Letting go means letting go of the need to let go. Sometimes letting go means holding on. I hope you're figuring this out now. Letting go is embracing change. Except for when it's not. Sometimes letting go is embracing routine. It's not an abdication of control. Except for when it is. Just when you think you've let go in one area, you find there are two sides to it. It's giving yourself permission to be wrong and learn how to recover as you go on a quest to find out who you are and what you love.

Letting go is unlearning. It's deconstruction of an internal structure that has broken down or perhaps can't handle the weight of what it now bears. This painfully beautiful process is best displayed in how obsessed we are with home renovations on HGTV. Unlearning prepares us to receive new instruction. Instruction creates an internal structure that causes us to live and move and have our being in Christ, and function as a person led by the fire of His presence without fear. Deconstruction often comes from a disillusionment at what was previously taught. If we don't let go of our bitterness we will let fear keep us from new information. This is jaded cynicism that takes a deconstructed heart to a place from which it may not recover easily. If you're a leader, deconstruction is a tough and lonely journey to invite others to take, so don't expect everyone to jump on your bandwagon. But those who will walk with you, whether they agree with your perspective or not, those people are ones you can trust. If you find a spouse you can take this journey with, that is a treasure indeed.

Allow me to say one more thing before circling back to this first person you marry. Recovering from deconstruction with an internal structure forged in the crucible of transformation, takes being surrendered to sonship again. It's not allowing fear to keep you from being a student once again and forevermore. As you receive information, you decide what to allow to form within you. A disillusioned heart in too much pain or confusion to trust, will hear a sermon very differently than the person at rest in the Father's embrace. Pay attention and consider how you hear another and ask yourself if love and grace is the filter through which you are receiving instruction and information. This is not a love-inflicted blindness to bad ideas, but it seeks the understanding of another every bit as much as it longs to be understood.

Letting go of the person you think they are, is giving them freedom to be. Marriage wouldn't be seen as confining if freedom to become was put on display. On some days, you will be faith and your spouse will be doubt. If differences divide people in your world, and you don't want to implode your marriage on some poorly defined perspective of unity, then you'll appreciate the diversity of thought that shatters your pristine and perfect idea.

One day, I had a friend call me in a fit of panic declaring to me that his wife had just nonchalantly decided she didn't want to be married anymore. Most of the time, this scenario is cause for alarm, but in this case, I felt at peace. I knew this girl and as a young married woman she was fully committed to the idea of marriage. When it got old, she felt a change coming on and interpreted this as a need to get out of the marriage. She loved being with her friends and going out most nights. Her husband was building a career and making sure her needs were covered. He had taken on a role and she wasn't quite ready to play the part he had envisioned in his head. I visited with her and realized what was going on in her mind. She was simply admitting that she didn't like being married all the time. I think most people can relate on various levels. But what she didn't want to be was the person in his head that she could never live up to. That newly discovered free spirited human was the person she wanted to be. She looked back on her process and began to realize that she was undergoing a transformation of perspective and personality that often comes with the passing of time. When they realized that they were just going through a time of change and growth, they recommitted to continue the journey together.

We're either going to journey alone or together, but as long as you have a pulse, you will be on a journey of changing from glory to glory. Change together and you'll have someone to hug and hold you with every glorious finish line you cross throughout the process of mastering the art of letting go.

Chapter 3

A Masterpiece With Issues

*"There is no pride in loving the art of an artist, for to
love the work of His hands is to love the artist whose
hands formed the work."*
Bill

The second person you marry is the person they think they are.

The power we have over another person is downright scary. You
can play God with people's emotions, and that kind of power is
something we abuse too easily. Someone you love has the power to
make you believe that you're beautiful or ugly, just by the way
they look when they see you.

Do you ever argue with your spouse about their view of
themselves? Do they look in the mirror, disappointed by what they
see? Do they constantly put themselves down and carry themselves
as if they have little worth? We rarely see ourselves as amazing as
the person who loves us does. If a woman deeply believes she's
unattractive, unproductive, and worthless, her language may reflect
that. Her husband had better not agree with her, as a matter of fact,
the success of this relationship is dependent upon his ability to
argue her into a better perception of herself. The problem with this
arrangement is that the success of the marriage is now based upon

disagreement. He will work diligently to convince her she's wrong, and she may believe him for a few moments here and there. But the necessity to reinforce that view is constant. Eventually, for the relationship to be sustainable, they'll have to come to some agreement, because negativity wears you down to the point that you feel like you're being stung to death by one bee. The connection of love that intrigued and attracted you to one another can begin to fade, and before you realize it, you're too tired to care about each other anymore.

It's in these moments that another amazing person can enter the picture and you find yourself divided in heart, loyal to one, but loving the other. In the greater agreement lies the greater connection, and that depth of connection can convince you that being happy with someone you agree with is better than being committed to someone you have failed to convince. I believe much of the self-downing people do is manipulative, attempting to get their spouse to cough up rare and valuable words of affirmation. But this manipulation can backfire badly, for any communication that is based upon a deceptive agenda works against intimacy, even if you get the words you were starving to hear. On the flip side of low self esteem is the spouse whose ego and self-centeredness also damages the relationship and shuts down true intimacy. That's a whole other issue.

LOVING THE ART IS LOVING THE ARTIST

I heard Kris Vallotton share a similar illustration to the one I'm about to share. It had a profound impact on how I saw humanity. Imagine that you walk into a museum filled with priceless works of art. As you step near to look closely at a painting, you see a man standing close by the work, gazing at it himself. You begin to

25

critique the work, tearing down the choice of color or texture, making clear that it does not please you in any way, and demeaning its value by saying, "I wouldn't take that home if they gave it to me." In all of this, the man close by stands silent. Moving on to a painting you prefer far more, you notice the name of the artist in the bottom right corner of the painting and just as you notice the name, another person approaches the man and calls him by the same name.

You would suddenly realize a very embarrassing and profound truth; that without realizing it, you were indirectly attacking this man by directly attacking his creation. The painting did not paint itself, which is what makes it so easy to criticize. You can tell a painting that it's worthless, and it would have nothing to speak back to you other than to reflect the choices and brushstrokes of its creator. The same is true when we demean ourselves. When we view ourselves with contempt, we indirectly attack our Creator. There is no pride in loving the art of an artist, for to love the work of His hands is to love the artist whose hands formed the work.

To see your spouse as a reflection of the artist, a unique masterpiece, an individual expression of the Creator, this is to look beyond the abuse of the years, to look past the effect of self-inflicted choices, the scratches and scars of moving through life, and to see what the artist always envisioned. Paintings of great value often go through painstaking restoration processes, and so it is with us.

Perhaps God has brought you into a person's life to restore the colors and hues and bring to life the redemptive story that the artist always wanted to tell. We enter another's life and take the brush from the artist's hand, believing we could do better. And so we
26

work to put our own touches on the art, with the desire to reflect ourselves in them. It's an interesting observation to realize that the heart not surrendered to God will strive to make another in our own image. We marry someone with opposite traits and characteristics, attracted by their diversity and differences, and then we spend the rest of our lives trying to change them. All we're doing is attempting to make them in our likeness. This is futility, for it is not the intention of the artist to hand over his masterpiece to you to change or alter, but rather to care for and protect. This much you can be confident in, that the artist is still creating. Your job is to give Him room and space to do His work by getting out of the way, listening for His voice, and learning to see what He sees. To spend time with the artist is to learn why He creates the way that He does, and when you know His heart, you will see His image and likeness in every single one of His works.

> *When we view ourselves with contempt, we indirectly attack our Creator.*

King David said, in Psalm 139, "Where can I go to flee from Your Spirit, or where can I go to hide from Your Presence…" As you move through life, see His art. Listen to their stories and you'll appreciate the brushstrokes of His kindness, provision, love, and grace. You'll see tears and scars from abuse and neglect. You'll see the fingerprints of people who had no appreciation for what they were handling. And you'll see the moments of healing and restoration as they were made new, time and time again. With every passing moment the picture is clearer and richer, and you might find that you love the work of His hands. This is a most precious expression of worship. For to fall in love with the art is to adore the artist.

Here are a few questions to ask yourself:

1. Have my words and thoughts toward myself been glorifying to God, my Creator?

2. Have my words and thoughts toward my spouse been glorifying to God, their Creator?

3. What are some positive, life-giving words I can say about myself?

4. What are some positive, life-giving words I can speak over my spouse?

Chapter 4

Learning to Love

"If your hatred for someone's past outweighs your love for them in the now, there's little hope for a positive future."
Bill

The third person you marry is the person they are, at this very moment, in their journey.

It has been said that every life is a book. As with any book, don't judge the story by the chapter you walked in on. Rather, recognize that your introduction into their story may be an invitation to contribute to their journey in such a way that you become an important part of helping them to write a glorious conclusion.

Here's how I know we are spiritual. We have the capacity to experience pleasure and pain. Not just physical, but on a much deeper level. If there was no ability to feel pleasure or pain, how would we determine whether something was good or bad? But because these deep "touches" exist, we can then question the motivation of why we would inflict either on ourselves or each other. Not every pleasure is good, just as not every pain is bad, so we can't discover motive simply based on what is being experienced at the moment. If all pleasure was good and all pain was bad, then the surgeon would be called evil and the prostitute would be called holy. With the ability to experience pain and remember it, we can adopt the identity of a victim, and question the motive of everyone, or worse, assume the motive of evil as the core of all. The story it seems, is that we are all on a journey to learn to love, to learn to bring into each other's lives a pleasure of inclusion, acceptance, and pure self-giving, other-centered, affection. Every relationship, every connection, gives us the chance to learn to love. The moment it turns from selfless to selfish, everything goes wrong and the story

> *We are all on a journey of learning to love.*

takes a tragic turn. Disconnection and disunity are the result, and we are never more blind to the divine nature within us than when we make division our purpose. We have then failed to learn the lesson that I believe God is trying to teach us all. Have you learned to love?

Every person is on a journey of pain and pleasure, conflict and conquest, ecstasies and heartbreak, with soaring highs and plunging lows. The lows bring with them a sense of isolation, causing you to feel as if nobody in the universe has ever been as broken as yourself. It's a comforting loneliness being in a cold, dark valley with warm memories. But there's no deeper loneliness than the sense that you are not loved. To be loved is to be woven into the tapestry of another's heart, and it's there that you find a place you can call home.

Everyone stands between the tension of the past and the future. What you have done, what you have done with what you did, and what you need to do now; all of these are conflicts of interest. For to be interested in one is to be led to the others until you're caught in an unbroken circle of unproductive confusion. The person that your spouse is right now is dealing with what has been done. Maybe they've done some things you hate. The question you need to ask yourself is do you hate what they've done more than you love them? If your hatred for their past outweighs your love for them as a present person, there's little hope for a positive future. Dealing with the past is never an easy task. One way to come to a place of forgiveness is to accept that things may never be the same as they were, but they can be better.

We all live in story. And God seems content with our creativity. The endless universes are the stories we create within the singular story of God. We are the artistic expression of the master storyteller. We can experience and inflict pleasure and pain, and we call those experiences good and evil. No matter the experiences we have, the conclusion of all of our stories is usually a group hug. Think about it. Every shared experience, whether a play, a support group, a football game, a quest, a test, or a wartime battle, the culmination of a shared experience usually finds closure when someone opens their heart and arms, and people embrace.

You may be realizing that the topic of this book has shifted a bit and you might be thinking, "Bill, I thought this book was going to be about fixing my partner. You're supposed to tell me what's wrong with them and tell me how to overpower the things I don't like so they'll become the person I made up in my mind at the beginning." Before you can judge the journey of another, learn to appreciate where your own journey has brought you. If you can be grateful for where the journey has brought you, then you can find hope for where the journey is bringing you. And if you can find hope for your own future, perhaps you can find hope for the future of the person you married, no matter where they are today.

KEEP GOING

When we lived in Hawaii, I was shocked one day when a police detective told me that it was not unusual for people to come to paradise to end their lives. Suicide is the destination option of a perspective of hopelessness. When the drugs and alcohol no longer numb the pain of a lifetime of getting it wrong, good people without hope sometimes make the choice to end the story. It's selfish, but a different kind of selfishness, because rather than a quest for pleasure, it's motive is often to stop the pain. Some who attempted suicide and failed, have said that setting their partners free was the driving force. But far from setting them free, the weight of hopelessness and pain is passed along. Selfishness, in any form, blinds us to the feelings of another and we lose all perspective of how we are being experienced.

Even people surrendered to God can move from victorious to suicidal.

The prophet Elijah had just come from one of the most dramatic victories in the history of humanity, where the literal fire of God showed up to validate Elijah's word and calling. The prophets of Baal were decimated and Elijah was now in a most triumphant position. Yet shortly after this immense victory, we find Elijah alone, depressed, questioning his life, and ultimately praying for death. God takes Elijah on a journey through a series of manifestations that, even though He sends them, He is not "in" them. God's presence shows up in a still small voice. You might think that a suicidal prophet who is a hero to the people of God would deserve a stay in rehab, or at least a weekend at the Four Seasons and a day at the spa, but God lets Elijah take a journey to a much more necessary destination. The end of himself. For all of the details of this important story, read 1 Kings 18-19.

If you ever find yourself at a place of hopelessness, and you just want the journey to stop, please re-read this section again and know that you're not alone. Keep going. Don't quit. Never give up. These may seem trite, so let me appeal to two words used often in the Bible. *Take courage.* It literally is an encouragement to confront fear and face what's challenging you. It's an invitation to rest and rely on the strength of another. The reckless grace of Jesus Christ is a constant resource of power and love. He is fully aware of every challenge you're facing in the present. He's not cowering at the challenge ahead of you, even if you've created it. His grace will take you through to the other side where victory is already yours. Take courage and don't lose heart. The story is not over until the author says so.

Who you are at this moment in time, and who your spouse is at this moment in their journey does not dictate the end result. If things seem hopeless, anchor your heart into the heart of Christ, lock eyes with the One who sees clearly, fix your focus on the love of God that changes everything, the kindness of God that leads to repentance, and His arms of compassion. Learning to love sometimes takes us through difficulties that try to convince us that there's nothing but darkness ahead, but that is a lie.

Take a few minutes to talk with God about learning to love. How have the circumstances in your life and marriage challenged your ability to love? How have those same circumstances expanded your ability to love?

Chapter 5

Fully Known Forever

"God knew you before He formed you, and what He knew is what He knows, and what He knows is who you really are."
Bill

The fourth person you marry is the person they are becoming.

If you're more than what others see, more than what you see, and more than you have currently become, then who in the cosmos are you?

God said a most remarkable thing to the prophet, Jeremiah. "I knew you before I formed you." So then, your origin was in the heart and mind of God, and it's this same God that, in Christ, is dedicated to complete the good work He began in you. He is fully invested in and committed to the glorious completion of you being filled with Him, who fills all in all.

This last person is the person God knows, and the person God has always known. He's not reacting with cringing groans to your blind badness or reeling from the shocking choices of your most toxic mindset. He, Who is the Author and Finisher of your faith, is not threatened by your sin. He has both the power and the will to refuse sin the right to cling to your account. This is how He preserves who you are becoming, even as He is completing the work He began in you. God made up His mind about you before you were ever here to make a choice that might delight or disappoint Him. He who knows the end from the beginning is committed to the completion of the creation that the good work of His heart and hands is forming within you. To even begin to see yourself as God sees you, and to understand how our Father's love transcends a helpless sense of disappointment, we need to turn our attention to the invention of time.

When God thought of you…

It's often said that God is outside of time, and for us who only know linear progression that moves at one speed, in one direction, that's a hard concept to understand. Most everything we read in the Scriptures shows a picture of a Creator who, though the inventor of time, experiences the progression of it as we do. Every time you read the common phrase, "…then God…" you can see that at a point within time, God took action. We can't begin to consider an existence of a singular eternal now without bringing all movement, progression, and unfolding wisdom and understanding to a complete end. Outside of time there would be no growth, no creativity, no surprises, no disappointments, no death, no life. No life? Well, if there was no life, there was no living, for all living involves movement, requiring space and time to move within.

Perhaps you thought that the best God could do was to simply forgive and forget our past and remove it from us as far as the east is from the west. But I believe that His redemptive power can do even more than forgive you. He can restore you to the original righteousness of holy innocence.

Consider this, that the One who knows the end from the beginning created the very beginning that began the turning of the wheels of the cosmos, and movement and momentum of moments was the byproduct. "In the beginning, God created..." He created a beginning, and that beginning was a part of the creation that He declared was good, and even, very good. What I'm hoping you're aware of is that time is a blessed and good gift. It's not a prison where we must die in order to escape. I believe there is time in heaven. The concept of eternity is not that we are outside of time, but that we are promised an existence that does not end. If the time of your living has been filled with pain, then the concept of continuing that pain indefinitely is hardly anything to throw a party about. But the promise of heaven is that we will see the redemption of every moment of the pain of the past, and the promise of a future where violence and betrayal will be ultimately overcome with peace and love. It's the very presence of Jesus Christ that makes this possible. Ecclesiastes 3:15 reveals a stunning perspective. *That which is has been already, and that which will be has already been, for God seeks what has passed by.* God is looking to redeem the past. Perhaps there are some spots in your past or your spouse's past that seem impossible to redeem.

How does He redeem the past moments we've already lived?

In the Old Testament story of Abraham and Sarah, the word of the Lord came to Abram one day and revealed that he was going to father children, more numerous than the stars. The problem is that he had no children, and he was old. When he told his wife, Sarah, what God said, she laughed at the word. Then she came up with one of the worst ideas in human history. She told Abraham to have a child with their servant, Hagar. Abraham went along with the plan, and Hagar got pregnant with Ishmael. Sarah eventually got pregnant too, with Isaac. These two brothers of one father eventually begat two nations who fight to this very day, and we get a ringside seat of this sibling rivalry on the daily news. Middle East conflict is between two brothers, both blessed by God, who refuse to love one another. Eventually someone will have to take Jesus' command to love our enemies to heart, but it's difficult to embrace a word and yet reject the one who gave it. Isaiah 19:23-25 prophecies that this peace and unity will in fact one day be a glorious reality.

Remember Sarah's initial response of laughing at the word of the Lord? In Hebrews 11, there is a beautiful rundown of Biblical characters who exhibited great faith. Such great faith, in fact, that it gave them a perspective beyond the span of their own lifetime. They began to live, affecting a generation they would never see. Hebrews 11 includes Sarah in this list, and doesn't seem to recount her response, but instead implies that she trusted and believed God. So now we have a problem. If the writer of Hebrews is lying about the historical facts, then we have a major problem with the integrity of the Scriptures. I don't believe this is the case. I believe the writer of Hebrews was being led by the Holy Spirit. And here in this moment, we get a rare glimpse behind the veil of locked, linear time into how Heaven sees our history. The implication is that the redemption and justification of our lives doesn't just create blank spots in the historical record, but that the record is rewritten as it ought to have been. That's where we see

> *God doesn't just redeem your past. He can rewrite your history.*

God having the creative ability to move in every direction on the timeline on which we ride like a roller coaster.

God can stop the sun and yet allow life to continue to progress. God can move backwards and forwards on the timeline, and like a producer composing a piece of music, He can go back and re-record a piece that needs some remixing. This may seem far fetched from our vantage point, but do we believe that all things are possible? Then this must be possible. And if we believe this is possible, do we believe that He is that good? His desire to redeem us cannot be greater than our desire to redeem our own children. Ask yourself this question. "What would I do to redeem my children?" Then with that understanding, answer this question that Jesus asked the disciples. "Who do you say that I am?" What we believe about His heart and ability to redeem us is what infuses us with faith, hope, love, righteousness, peace, and joy.

In 1 Corinthians 3:21, the Apostle Paul wrote, "All things are yours..." He goes on to describe what encompasses all things. He mentions people, he mentions life and death, he throws in the entire cosmos, and then mentions the present and the future. But something is missing here. We know that time has more than two tenses. What about the past? If all means all, and your past isn't included, then what's going on here? The only possible solution to this dilemma is to realize that when God casts your sins as far as the east is from the west, it means one thing. Your past doesn't exist. At least not the past as we know it. Consider that the hope of a glorious future in Heaven comes with the revelation of a redeemed and remixed life story. Before we move on from the topic of time, let's consider two more sections of Scripture.

In John 16:33, Jesus reveals one of the reasons for His words. "These things I have spoken so that in Me you may have peace. In this world, you will have trouble. But be of good cheer, for I have overcome the world." Anything that we "will have" is in the future. So Jesus reveals that the future has some challenges, and we all know this to be so. But apparently He has already overcome the world. Notice the time tenses here. Jesus reveals that whatever trouble is coming in our future, we don't need to fear or have any sense of foreboding. He has already equipped you with everything necessary to step into every challenge as an overcomer.

To bring us back to the topic of redemption of reputation and relationship, let's turn our attention to the awkwardly uncomfortable study of the woman caught in the act of adultery. I wrote about this in the book, Reckless Grace, so there's additional insight there, but for the topic at hand, let me offer you this. The religious leaders caught her in the act, so there was no option for her to deny her guilt. Jesus dismantled religious judgment until the executioners all walked away. He turned to her and asked a question in John 8:10-11. "Is there no one here to condemn you?" She responds, "No one, Lord." The word for Lord is the Greek word, Kurios, which simply means *master* or literally *he to whom a person or thing belongs, about which he has power of deciding.* The woman caught in adultery does not appear to beg for mercy. Perhaps she feels as though she deserves none. She doesn't appear to repent. Perhaps she's lost all hope. She sees the authority of Jesus, and she sees herself in His hands. She belongs to Him, and now He has the power of deciding. Here's His response. "Neither do I condemn you. Now go and sin no more." This is quite astonishing, not just in its content, but in its order. Logically, the command to perform precedes the reward of pardon. It would make more sense for Jesus to say, "Go and sin no more. And when

I see that you can obey what I've told you to do, then you will have no condemnation." But instead, He grants her grace without her earning it, and from that place of purity she is free to live without the bondage of sin. He clearly knows something about how grace and time can work together to reveal more redemptive power to save us than perhaps we ever thought possible.

God knew you before He formed you, and what He knew is what He knows, and what He knows is who you really are. You really only have one quest in this life, and that's to see who you really are, and align with what our Father believes about you. None of this comes through striving. It only comes by surrender, and that's the rest of salvation by grace through faith. The entirety of Scripture closes with a line that appears in the final verses of Revelation, "...and the Spirit and the bride say, "'Come.'" Eventually, the Spirit and the bride declare the same thing. But I believe we don't need to push this off into the future. What if we started saying the same thing now? What if we could perceive the voice of the Lord and say yes to it? What if we let He who sits on the throne of our hearts speak from His own abundance and let His words be the abundance of our heart from which we speak? And what if we, speaking out of the abundance of a surrendered heart, find ourselves transformed in the process?

Who you are becoming is who you've always been. It's who you were always meant to be. And it's probably not who you have known before. 1 Corinthians 13:12 hints to this beautiful reality and the Message renders it brilliantly. *"We don't yet see things clearly. We're squinting in a fog, peering through a mist. But it won't be long before the weather clears and the sun shines bright! We'll see it all then, see it all as clearly as God sees us, knowing him directly just as he knows us!"* You are fully known by God right now. He's not waiting for you to reveal to Him who you are. I believe God is wanting to reveal to you what He has always known. He's just waiting for us to see, believe, and agree with what He sees. When we see what He sees, we won't say "Go! Get away. Get out of my sight!" We'll say, "Come! At last. The treasure hidden within you is fully revealed and you are complete in Him."

No matter how incomplete you feel on your journey right now, the Father knows you fully complete. Consider the mind melting quantum reality of Colossians 2:9-10, which says, "*In Christ, the fullness of the Godhead dwelt in a body. And, in Him, you have been made complete.*" Did you catch the time tense there? In Christ, you **have been** made complete. It's already an eternal reality, in Christ. Ted Dekker and I wrote about this in greater detail in "The Forgotten Way." You can't take away from something complete and have it remain complete, unless that which is taken away was never meant to be there to begin with. Christ has taken our sin away. Yet you remain complete. So sin has never been your identity. Like barnacles on a ship, or garbage on the inside of a building, it's not a part of the original design. That which is taken away in Christ was never meant to be you. In marriage, we must remember this about our spouse. There's something beautiful about being able to look at your spouse and see them in their original design.

The Holy Spirit will open your eyes to see Christ everywhere. King David said in Psalm 139, "Where can I go to flee from Your presence?" Even in the Old Covenant, a man came to the realization that God was harder to get away from than he thought. Fast forward to the New Covenant and in Colossians 3:11, the Apostle Paul declares of people that *Christ is all and in all.* Is this reality? It certainly doesn't look like it when you're watching people living for themselves with no regard for the presence of the Lord. Don't think this is something that we can shove into a future time period for which we have no present responsibility. Paul lost his self righteous judgment. He resigned his Pharisee persona and the gavel of condescension was dropped in the ditch a long time ago. He said in Colossians 1:17, *"He is before all things, and in Him all things hold together."* Notice the present tense? In Colossians 1:20 he wrote, *"And through Him to reconcile all things to Himself, having made peace through the blood of His cross;"* and again notice that in this verse, Paul spoke in a past tense.

You may wonder what that has to do with your marriage, so let's go ahead and apply this. (Before reading this section, please note that we will address abusive relationships a little later). Can you take a moment each day and ask God, "Who do You say that my spouse is?" Ask Him to reveal to you who He knows that they are.

Can you see Christ in your spouse before they ever see Him in themselves?

Forgive the glaring inconsistencies in your perspective of their present reality. Forgive the awkward shortfalls between the perspective of the Father and the actions of the human being before you. Look beyond the lies and the labels, the creature and the costume, and though you may have to squint a bit and ask for grace, see Christ. Even if they don't see Him in themselves, see Christ. The word *Christ* simply means *anointed one*. Can you find the oil of heaven's anointing beneath the surface of your spouse's costume? You may have to see Christ in someone long before they see Him in themselves, but that's the perspective revolution that we need. Jesus saw the woman caught in adultery as without condemnation when she felt judged as guilty. For her to go free, truly free, she needed to agree with His perspective.

42

Religious order had a perspective and Christ had another.

When Jesus told those who were about to stone her, "Let he who is without sin among you cast the first stone," did you ever wonder why He didn't take the time to really challenge them on their sin? After all, in that moment He was surrounded by sinners in need of a savior. Yet rather than reach out to each one in that moment, His attention and affection was fully on the one who was being crushed beneath the weight of condemnation. He wasn't giving His time to the self righteous. He was giving Himself to protect the condemned.

Do you see the reckless grace of Jesus Christ? Paul was taken by that, and in 2 Corinthians 5:14 he reveals that his motive and compulsion are love. "For the love of Christ compels us, having concluded this, that One has died for all, therefore all have died..." Paul has great confidence in the finished work of the cross.

See Christ in your spouse before they even see Him in themselves. When we can surrender to that perspective and lay down our own offense and frustration, then we will love like Christ. Our story and journey to realize this truth is one that you may be able to relate to, unless you've had a perfect marriage without any issues at all. And if that's the case, I can't wait to read your book. At this point, Traci will take the writing of the rest of this chapter to tell you a part of our story and how we arrived at this life changing and marriage altering revelation.

My Journey Through All Four Versions of Bill
by Traci

Who I thought he was.

I'll never forget the moment, at age seventeen, when I first heard Bill's manly voice on the other end of the line. "This is Bill Vanderbush. I don't know if you remember me or not." Of course I remembered! How could I not remember the name *Vanderbush,* let alone the face of that cute, gentle-spirited, big-brown-eyed neighbor-boy from childhood? At age five, we had made mud pies, pretended to be spies as we scoped out the neighborhood, and watched Looney Tunes while eating Eggo waffles together. Those memories were seared into me forever.

After Bill and his family moved away, we had the pleasure of seeing each other periodically throughout our childhood years. A few years would pass in between our visits, but somewhere around the age of sixteen, we began writing each other. I recall staring at the photo he sent me of himself kicked back on the couch, holding a book, peering over his right shoulder at the camera. He had obviously mastered the art of the 1980's "smolder," with eyes piercing the core of my being. Bill fit right in with those handsome teen heartthrobs like Kirk Cameron and Ralph Macchio. *Hmm.* I studied that photograph for days as I marveled over the transformation of the little boy I once knew.

A year after receiving that photograph, the sound of his voice delighted me on the phone. Just those first four words out of his mouth, "This is Bill Vanderbush," awakened the innocence that I had lost throughout high school. He and I ended up meeting the next day, and by the third day, we had pledged our undying love to

44

each other. Within a month, Bill was off to Czechoslovakia where he would spend three long months, serving a mission and building a church. *Wow! My boyfriend is a missionary. How cool is that?*

I had dated several boys throughout high school and experienced heartbreak several times. My heart longed for deep relationship and connection, but it seemed I was the only one interested in such a thing. But with Bill, I believed I had found perfection. *If he loves God as much as he does, and he's so passionate about sharing the Gospel, he'll never disappoint me in any way.*

"He will never disappoint me in any way." That's a ton of pressure to put on another human being, yet I placed all of my security, value, and worth in someone that I imagined him to be: perfect, perfect, perfect, absolutely infallible, and eternally unselfish. We made it to our wedding day (he was 18 and I was 19) and he hadn't disappointed me yet. While he is quite amazing, the very first moment of disappointment came shortly after we were married. While running to the car during a heavy rainstorm, hand-in-hand, I felt so cherished. *Look at that. He's taking care of me, escorting me to the car safely.* He opened the door and quickly jumped in, and shut the door, leaving me outside to be soaked! Yes, I never let him forget that moment. Who I thought he was may have become slightly warped in that moment.

Who he thought he was.

At age seventeen, Bill would have described himself as being totally confident and sure that he could accomplish anything and be whatever he wanted to be. He saw no obstacles ahead of him; only opportunities to rise. He was ready for life, on the edge of heading out to experience every place and every culture in the world. If you've seen the movie, Catch Me If You Can, with Leonardo DiCaprio, that would give you a good idea of Bill's level of confidence. He was fearless and saw no task as being beyond his ability. I can vouch for this, as I watched him work numerous positions throughout the years that he was not qualified for, yet he excelled.

Who did I believe I was? At age seventeen, I had vowed that my life would be very different from the lives of my family members. Not that their lives were not good; it was just that they had to work hard to overcome obstacles created by their choices. My mom was fifteen years old when she became pregnant with me. Yes, fifteen years old! Miraculously, she and my dad have remained married all of these years, which is pretty amazing. They paid a price, though. Life has been difficult for them, to say the least, but I'm so thankful they stayed the course and raised their children the best they could. That's an accomplishment and a testimony to being selfless.

Imagine this contrast:
Me, a child of a young, hippie couple who lived in a trailer park...
Bill, a child of a middle-aged couple who were traveling evangelists...
Me, a child of a belly dancer...
Bill, a child of a preacher...

For some of my mom's side of the family, marital issues and divorce were a common theme. I hated it, so I decided that would never be a part of my story. I was determined that my marriage would never suffer. I envisioned an eternal, blissful, almost puritanical, perfect Christian marriage that would shine as an example to the multitudes and be the shift in the family line that would break the curse of relational difficulty (hysterical, right?).

46

Imagine the mix of a deeply introverted, naïve, hopeful, young woman who lacked self esteem, joined with an extremely extroverted, overly confident, young man with plenty of self esteem to take over the world. Both starry-eyed and optimistic about a bright future, we embarked on a new chapter, believing that we knew who we were. Little did we know the challenges that would come to threaten our identity and our worth. Little did we know that we would come to discover different facets of ourselves that we never knew existed; or perhaps that circumstances and disappointments created within us.

Who we thought we were would certainly be called into question.

Who he was, once upon a time…

Vulnerable moment: It was a heated argument; a day of disappointment, disillusionment, and I was left wondering if I was really loved at all. Bill appeared bewildered, confused, and also wondered if he was loved by me. How does a seemingly good relationship end up in such a moment? In such a mess? I recall going for a jog to let off steam. I cried as I ran, expressing both hurt and anger as I griped at God for allowing the confusion. After all, how can two people live their lives focused on God and ministry, and be allowed to fall into a trap of miscommunication and confusion? The events of the day evoked chaos in my soul. I decided the best solution would be to build a wall around my heart, be stoic, and lose my typical vulnerability. I was mad. Anger was often the defense mechanism of my choosing in order to prevent tears of sadness, which is not a good practice.

That night, I did not speak to Bill. I knew he was sad, regretful, and wondering if our relationship was in severe trouble. My silence was punishment. As I crawled into bed next to him, lying back-to-back, I hoped he could feel the daggers projecting from my soul. As I tried to close my eyes and brush off the trauma of the day, I refused to speak to God because I was mad at Him, too. The clock ticked, seemingly as a reminder that I only had seconds to turn this ship around before it crashed upon the rocks. I remained cocooned in offense and judgment. Suddenly, and without warning, the Holy Spirit's voice shook my insides with this gentle, yet firm command: "Hold that man." Those three words shocked me. *What? Hold that man? Hold that man who isn't showing me love? Hold that man who's been a huge jerk? Hold that man that caused me pain?* Yet I knew those words were clearly from the Father, and I felt that it would be my choice as to whether or not we would survive. It would be my choice to hold that man or not. So, I rolled over and wrapped my arms around Bill. I immediately felt his body relax as if the weight of the world lifted, and to my great surprise, I was flooded with love and compassion. There was an instant, holy connection that broke through the chaos and confusion. It was indescribable and it made no sense.

What if I had chosen not to obey those three words, *Hold that man?* My carnal eyes could only see the negative and the disillusionment, but eternal eyes carried the power to see my husband as God created him to be. God knew there was more to him than eyes could see. My obedience to His voice ripped away the blinders and helped me to see in Christ; to see as He sees, to see my husband through the eyes of Love Himself.

If you have been in a relationship for a long period of time, whether marriage, friendship, and/or any type of companionship, you have probably watched that person go through various changes and seasons of life. This journey of life is a canvas of discovery and experience. Some experiences are out of our control, while we can steer other experiences. It's usually the ones that are out of our control that tend to shape our belief systems. When our beliefs about life shift, our filters for doing life are changed.

Where your spouse is right now may not line up with who they **really** are. The person you marry may be one way today, but how will life change them tomorrow? Will they face something that will challenge their heart, thoughts, and beliefs? Will the challenges change them for better, or for worse? There are so many questions we cannot answer.

How will life change you? Have you ever imagined certain scenarios and how you would respond? Bill and I believed we would always think and feel a certain way about things, but we found ourselves facing challenges that shaped and formed us into something we never imagined. Sometimes those changes were positive while some situations brought out the worst in us. When the worst arises, that's usually when couples call it quits and bail out. In those darkest moments, are you actually seeing who you and your partner really are?

When I say *really are*, I'm talking about who their Father created them to be; who He dreamed of before we ever took our first breath on this earth.

Do you carry grace to release to the one you love as they go through different stages of life; stages of joy, laughter, sorrow, doubt and anger? Do you carry grace to release to yourself as your heart, soul, and mind are touched by the issues of this world? If

49

we do not carry an attitude of grace and premeditated forgiveness, we won't always be able to live with who our spouse is right now. And without grace and forgiveness, they won't always be able to live with who we are right now.

Each of our lives is a book, and the moral of the story is: don't judge a person by the chapter you walk in on.

This journey of life is a canvas of discovery and experience.

When I read the words of Romans 8:29, I often ponder the phrase, "For those whom He foreknew, He also predestined to become conformed to the image of His own Son..." I understand that there is more to that section of scripture, but those particular words arrest my heart with the glory of God and all that He desires, because who does He **not** know? He foreknew all that He created. Top that off with 2 Peter 3:9 which says, "...God is patient toward you, not wishing for any to perish but for all to come to repentance." Based on those two scriptures alone, I believe it is safe to say that our spouses were created for a glorious destiny: to be conformed to the image of God. The Father wills that all would know Him. Not everyone has that awakening, but it helps us to navigate through rough waters if we can look at our spouse as one who is destined to know the Father. Seeing who they are becoming guides us in how we treat them.

I am personally very thankful for every moment when my husband continued loving me even when the worst of my insecurities and issues came to the surface. Bill could have easily written me off and marked me as being "that" person. It's also true that I could have written Bill off as something he wasn't, during the times when he acted like someone other than the man I believed I had married. If we label or mark each other by our lowest, darkest moments, then we have gone blind to who the person will become by the grace of God. This is one of the great mysteries of God's amazing grace: the power of that grace to transform the most unlikely heart. It is the power of God to take what the enemy used for destruction, and create a beautiful, redemptive story that overpowers the ugliness of the past.

In regards to abusive situations:

There are some dangerous situations where a person needs to remove themselves from a marriage. Please understand that even though God can redeem an abuser, we would not advise someone to remain in an abusive situation. Sometimes a person needs to leave a situation and continue to pray for the person from the safety of boundaries. We have witnessed a couple of decades of covert abuse in the life of a loved one who finally took the steps to escape the abuse that she kept hidden. There are cases, like with extreme, covert narcissism, and/or sociopathic issues in which the abuser cleverly appears to be a wonderful person to those on the outside, but at home, exercises control that's riddled with lies, manipulation, and scare tactics. Abusers have a way of disempowering their spouse through words and actions, leaving them to feel as if they have no ability to escape the situation. Belittling, gaslighting, making their partner feel crazy, requiring admiration, feeling entitled, being self-absorbed, and uncaring about your feelings, these are all red flags. In these scenarios, sometimes all the prayers and efforts to make things better do not work because the abuser refuses to acknowledge their own issues. We have known people over the years who exhausted every resource while facing a spouse's relentless abuse cycles (addiction is sometimes involved, which is a whole other story). We've witnessed miraculous turnarounds and interventions that changed the course of the couples' lives, and we've also witnessed the breakdown and separation of marriages, which were necessary. Either way, the grace of God is available to you, and His power to heal hearts is real.

If you're suffering under the weight of abuse, please seek professional help and knock on every door until someone listens to you. You're not alone. And this is not the end of your story, or your spouse's story. Love never fails.

Chapter 6

Love is Within You

"You are the expression of the love of God to one another."
Bill

Love is the desire of the nations. The quest of all mankind. The indescribable goal of the human spirit. The gift everyone wants, yet struggles to feel worthy of. Even to the point where one day, a desperation arises within the heart and erupts with a revelation that I absolutely, unconditionally, without reservation or inhibition deserved to be loved because...

And there is where the inevitable pause steals the wind out of the lover's sails, stalls the passion of the heart, and quiets the voice of the spirit with the lying shush of unworthiness. And as long as the quest is for a feeling, a concept, an ideology, a philosophy, the pause has a voice. For love is none of these.

Love is a person. The personification of God, the Word made flesh, the living, breathing lover of our soul, Jesus Christ. He is the origin, the embodiment, the catalyst, the source, authentic Love Himself. And He is so appropriately called in the Scriptures the "Desire of the Nations." So your search then has brought you together; where then is Jesus?

The Bible unveils a great mystery that is not Christ in Heaven, but Christ within you, the Hope of Glory. It is the revelation of your identity as being in Christ, Who is love, that will continue to unveil the lover's heart within you. He is lacking in nothing, so nothing is lacking within you. And yet His gifts are not given in response to that which you are lacking. He gives because He is good. And so you will give to one another, not because the other is lacking, but because the goodness of Love's gift needs no reason to be given. Love gives because it longs to express itself. And so the longing on the heart of God in creating you was not born of lack, but of love.

You are Love's expression to one another. You are God's expression to this world that is filled with humanity that has become famous for judgment, when we were created to be famous for love. And in loving, we express His workmanship. The Bible, in Ephesians 2:10 says you are His workmanship. That is the poiema of God, meaning an artistic, created masterpiece. And this I declare over you today: That the poem of God would be recited in your lives. In your words, your gaze, your life. That the poem of Love's heart would be given a voice in this union from this day forward. And that you would make Him, once again, famous for love.

Traci's Challenge

Doesn't it seem impossible at times to walk in love, especially when you become so familiar with someone? Being witness to their daily shortcomings, ups and downs, and normal human functions (I mean, who pictures their perfect, ideal lover sitting on the toilet?); the closeness can steal away the attraction and the feelings of excitement. I, Traci, once listened to a conversation with a polished preacher who told his leadership team about how he wouldn't get close to anyone in his congregation because "familiarity breeds contempt." I thought about that statement and considered that he was correct. The closer and more familiar we become with people, eventually, something will taint their perspective of us and contempt would be the result. I lived by that statement for a time, and then I realized just how wrong it was.

Awhile back, as I struggled with a friend's less-than-desirable behavior, I prayed and lamented. This conversation began in my head with God:

"Traci, you must be grace to this person."

"I cannot. It's too much. You do it Yourself, God. You're pretty good at that grace stuff anyway. Besides, haven't You heard that familiarity breeds contempt? Why get close to people?"

"That is not true. In an atmosphere of grace, familiarity breeds love."

His words struck me to the core as I was then faced with the decision to come into agreement with Jesus' sacrifice for that person. Would I be a grace-giver? I didn't feel I had it within me to be a grace-giver to that person, but God's voice rang deep inside of me once more: *"Your name is Courageous Grace."*

And it is true. Grace requires courage. Giving grace takes strength and bravery as we lay our hearts bare before one another, risking familiarity. The words I heard in my spirit, "In an atmosphere of grace, familiarity breeds love," rang deep. I pondered those words and began to think about how Christ loved us when we did not deserve love. "But God demonstrates his own love toward us, in that while we were still sinners, Christ died for us." Romans 5:8 blows my mind because God was familiar with man's ways. He knew how wicked, how disrespectful, and how selfish we could be, yet He came anyway, and wrapped Himself in the very flesh we wear. He touched, tasted, and smelled the things of earth, experiencing joy, sadness, turmoil, and submitted Himself to the brutality of His own creation, all because He loved us. Despite becoming familiar with man, Christ did not grow in contempt; instead, He responded to man with "Father, forgive them. They know not what they do." And He embraced humanity with relentless love. "God was in Christ reconciling the world to Himself, not counting their wrongdoings against them." That is courageous grace!

2 Corinthians 5:19 is an example of a perfect response to becoming familiar with others. Instead of contempt, we lay down our lives. This seems counteractive and completely goes against the grain, yet it's the way of the Father who is Love. Had Jesus not been willing to be courageous grace, we would not know the glorious way of Love.

In regards to your spouse, when they are driving you crazy or you just aren't feeling the attraction, remember the reality that attraction and feelings of excitement ebb and flow throughout the years. When you don't feel the love, remember that Love lives within you, and you have the power to tap into that Love any time. Ask Love Himself to love your spouse through you, and just watch what happens. When we open our hearts and minds to the Lover of our souls and we courageously allow Him to demolish our insecurities, frustrations, and even our "rights," we find freedom to love in a way we didn't know was possible. When Bill and I have done this, we've experienced love and attraction all over again, on

56

a greater level. Just when you think you've experienced the depths of love with your spouse, you find there's more to be explored and known. Even the hardest, ugliest parts of our relationship became seed for growing a deeper love, so don't be afraid of becoming too familiar. Intimacy is made up of vulnerability. And vulnerability takes courage. Laying your cards on the table is one of the most liberating things you can do in your marriage. Bill and I have a "no secrets" policy. We spent the first seventeen years of marriage feeling that we had to hide certain feelings and experiences. Intimacy and secrets just don't mix. When we hit rock bottom and sought out a counselor to help us fix things, we learned about the power of openness and honesty. With grace in the atmosphere, we could freely lay all cards on the table. It may be scary, but it's one of the most powerful things you can do to grow your relationship.

This is possible because love lives within you. And when love lives within you, you're capable of doing death-defying acts. Perhaps our soul is born with a mission. That mission is the death-defying act called "to love." Some believe that man is born without the ability to love and that he must be taught how to love. I disagree. We were all created in love, by love, and for love, no matter what the life circumstances are that surround our beginnings and endings.

Every child longs to do the impossible. At some point in our lives, we dreamed of doing something beyond the ordinary…maybe flying, moving mountains, changing hearts, circumstances, or surroundings. Ultimately, we have longed to defy death. And certainly, love defies death. Love Himself defied death and conquered it eternally.

Since we were in Christ before the foundation of the world, it is in our DNA to walk deeper into this death-defying act of loving our spouse. Letting go of all that prevents us from loving them creates an open runway where, upon stepping out in faith, we learn that we have had wings all along. When you and your spouse just can't seem to pull it together, remember that Love lives within you. Tap into Him, and it is there that you can learn to fly together.

Chapter 7

Mastering Money

"It's time to lift the financial shame and launch into a new mindset."
Traci

I've witnessed it too many times: men and women sitting before us, tear-filled eyes, heads hung low with shame because of their financial situation. I've listened to men tell their stories of working overtime, tiring themselves to the point of misery as they struggle to keep a roof over their children's heads, to keep them fed, to maintain their dental care and medical needs. "I'm working all the hours I possibly can, yet I'm barely able to pay all the bills," one strong man said as his chin quivered. "I'm so embarrassed. How will my kids even go to college?"

I've watched mothers strive to pick up the messes left behind by men who broke their promises. These women balance motherhood and fatherhood, working jobs, keeping house, and hoping to be there for children when they become sick. Employer's demands push them and override their ability to spend precious time with their kids. Shame settles on them like a wet blanket as they question themselves, doubting that they'll ever be able to succeed.

I've also known too many miracles in my own life and the lives of others, to be quiet. It's time to lift the financial shame and launch into a new mindset.

The majority of the first twenty-three years of our marriage was spent living on the edge financially. I must tell you that we know what it's like to stand in that W.I.C. line, we know what it's like to have to put groceries back on the shelf and remove items at the checkout, and we know what it's like to have a car (make that two) repossessed, and we know what it's like to be sued, to cry after hanging up a call from the bill collector, and we know what it's like to struggle to keep the electricity turned on. But what I can guarantee you is that we worked very hard the whole time, and God always did something miraculous. Our finances never added up on paper, but God made a way for the impossible, so much so, that people thought we were well-off financially, even when we weren't.

"The American Dream". It's a well-known concept that we all hope to acquire. Societal expectations loom and we adopt its demands as our commission for life, feeling that if we fall short of the expectations, we are failures. At an early age, we are set up to feel the weight of the dream: "What do you want to be when you grow up? What kind of job are you going to work? Where will you go to college? How are you going to make money?" I remember, as a high school student, bearing the weight of such questions that infused me with panic because all I really wanted to do was raise a family, love people and serve God. How would such things fit into the mold of living "the American Dream?"

Once I married Bill, the next set of questions loomed: "How will you pay for having children? Have you started putting money away for your children's college fund?" Put money away for college? We're just trying to keep the lights on and keep ourselves fed. Throughout life, the questions never cease: "Do you have health insurance, life insurance, and retirement set up?" Breathe. Breathe. Gosh, I barely have enough for gasoline to get me to work each day, but I can't let them know that.

Bill and I felt called to ministry. I have never met one person who went into ministry to make money. In fact, the majority of people who enter ministry are multi-vocational. Multiple jobs are required in order to sustain day-to-day living, especially when your family begins growing and you realize that children require more than you could have imagined. Medical, dental, eye care, food, clothing, etc. But one amazing fact stands true to this day; God truly supplied every need. And even when we lacked, somehow it all worked out. It was in those moments of lack that we learned Who our source is, and it also built our faith. We learned how strong we are, and even when the system of the world seemed to crush us, we learned humility and compassion. There was great value in each experience we had. And, oh yes, we fought many times about finances!

> *It is in moments of lack that we discover who our source is.*

Just a few of the jobs that Bill worked along the way were:

Youth Pastor (24/7)
Senior Pastor (24/7)
Associate Pastor (24/7)
Blockbuster Video Sales
House Painter

Zoo Membership Salesman
Credit Card Salesman
House Cleaner (for a celebrity)
Limousine Driver/Chauffeur
Bookstore Manager
Animation Studio Manager
Receptionist for Psychotherapy Office
Pizza Maker
Pizza Delivery Driver
A&R Rep for Grapetree Records (Rap Label)
Underwater Videographer
Industrial Shelving Installer
Wedding Videographer
Crepe Maker
…and many more.

Intertwined in that list would be the jobs that I worked in frame-making and glass cutting while Bill was a Senior Pastor. I also had the privilege of working with a foster care and adoption agency in which I got to help create families. But there are some funny stories in the mix, as well as some crazy risk-taking moments in our work history. One of my favorite stories was during our venture into cleaning the home of actress Sandra Bullock during construction. It's a hilarious story that I won't tell here because it's written in my book "Freedom From Financial Shame." If you want the nitty-gritty details of our highs and extreme lows, and a supernatural story that shifted everything for us, purchase the book on Amazon, and I promise, you will be glad you did! *Freedom From Financial Shame* has been a beautiful tool for releasing people into a new mindset that frees them from shame and lack.

The following is an excerpt from the book about how my mind-shift from poverty began:

Somewhere in the valley, there was a particular night when hopelessness weighed on me. As hard as I tried to be a great wife, mom, and minister, I found myself with a heavy heart, a skewed perspective, and my thoughts were jaded. We happened to be in Houston for a conference where I sat on the front row, unable to enter the joy of the event. The music played, people danced, but I felt darkness attempting to suffocate me. My mind wondered what was actually true. I didn't trust people. One of my closest friends had wounded me deeply, causing a mind-shift.

I found wealth in having great family and friends, but when disappointments came, I had to believe that God was the only one I could dream with, no matter how small or how big. Surely He was the only one I could completely, utterly trust, but even so, my soul wasn't 100% positive. There I was, on the floor of the sanctuary, lying on my back, body partially under a chair. While people around me cried with joy, I cried tears of sorrow. I hoped they would mistake my tears for the Lord doing a good work in me; and not recognize the tears for what they were…cries of desperation, questioning, and doubting. Before worship ended, I peeled myself off the floor and exited the sanctuary before anyone could try to hug me or engage me in conversation. I just needed to be alone. Alone with God.

I headed across the road and walked until I came to a series of office buildings. In the center was a peaceful fountain surrounded by weeping willows. My heart was drawn to a bench beneath one of the trees. I needed to cry with those trees. I ran my hands along the smooth wooden seat, deciding to recline on it. As I turned onto my side, my eyes rested on the water that flowed toward me before cascading down the sides. *He leads me beside still waters.* Those words rang deep within me. He leads me beside still waters. I gazed at the fountain, noticing the calm waters that rested along the edge once they had plummeted to their destination. *Maybe I'm like the waters.* I allowed peace to wash over me.

I looked at the grass around the fountain. *He makes me to lie down in green pastures.* I needed to feel the grass; touch it and experience it as a resting place, but I wasn't willing to leave the comfort of the bench. While the surface was hard, it was a comfort because it was holding me. I pondered how amazing it was that a living thing that God created had become useful in its death, and now brought me comfort. Could I possibly leave something behind that will bring comfort to someone after I'm long gone? Could this death of ego, death of certain dreams become a comfort to someone else in their own time of questioning?

He restores my soul. The words of Psalm 23 seemed to vibrate through my entire being. It was a psalm that I had memorized as a child. I won an award in school for reciting it from memory, yet I failed to understand the power of the words that I spoke. But now those words were deeply meaningful. *I think I get it.* The wind blew over me, the weeping willows swayed, I breathed in the comfort of my Father and spoke those words of long ago:

The Lord is my Shepherd. I shall not want.
In Him, I lack absolutely nothing. There is no need of anything.
He makes me to lie down in green pastures.
He wants me to rest. I have all I need.
He leads me beside still waters.
The raging waters that I thought would drown me are no longer raging. With God, I am at peace.
He restores my soul.
He loves my soul enough to revive it.

64

He leads me in the paths of righteousness for His name's sake.
He is true to His word. He sets everything right.
Though I walk through the valley of the shadow of death,
Death is only a shadow
I will fear no evil, for You are with me. Your rod and staff comfort me.
There is no reason to fear. His rod of power in my life, and His staff that guides me are for my good, not for my harm.
You prepare a table before me in the presence of my enemies,
Those who hurt me will see the Father pouring out His best and finest to me. He prepares a feast for His children. I can forgive them and invite them in to dine with me, so they will know that they were created to be my brothers and sisters.
He anoints my head with oil and my cup runs over.
He nourishes me with everything I need to live out my destiny, despite circumstances.
Surely goodness and mercy will follow me all the days of my life,
I cannot escape His goodness and mercy. They follow me, cleaning up the debris and making everything beautiful.
And I will dwell in the house of the Lord forever.
I will always be Home, wherever I am. Everything in my Father's house is mine. I have complete access, and there will never be a day when I do not have access to Him, His heart, and His ways.

That night at the fountain began a mind shift for me. There would always be enough. Whether in relationship, life challenges, finances, whatever it may be, there will always be enough. Either I believed it or I did not.

And certainly, that night, a powerful shift from a poverty mindset began. Since my thinking shifted, so have our experiences when it comes to finances.

Jesus said, "No one can serve two masters; for either he will hate the one and love the other, or he will be devoted to one and despise the other. You cannot serve God and wealth." Matthew 6:24 provokes a lot of thought in me about money. Wealth is not an evil thing. It's the love of money that's the root of all evil. Jesus made it clear that our love must be toward one or the other, not both. Now, if you think about the fact that Christ is within your spouse, envision that physical representation of God standing before you. Your spouse on the left. Money on the right. Which one will you love? Which one will you serve? Which one would you not want to live without?

When we determine not to love and serve money, but rather love and serve God and our spouse, we then have a solid foundation on which we can build a life together without the threat of falling apart over lack of money. When I began to understand this, our lives drastically shifted as we both began to believe God for anything, even when bank accounts, bills, and other things would scream, "Impossible!" With God, ALL things are possible. With God, nothing is impossible. Jesus said it, so either He was telling the truth, or He was a liar. Which do you believe? I believe what He said. Does ALL mean ALL? All things are possible. Living in this childlike trust, believing Him at His word, has given me the opportunity to see thousands of things happen that would not have happened had I stayed in the mindset of lack. We have to believe it before we see it.

We still may not have the entirety of the American Dream. We had no college fund for our kids. We may lack certain elements of what society says we should have, but honestly, lack is an illusion. God made everything possible. It's at our fingertips. It's within us.

Christ in you, the hope of glory (Colossians 1:27). When Jesus was asked by the Pharisees when the kingdom of God would come, He answered, "The kingdom of God does not come with observation, nor will they say, 'See here!' or 'See there!' For indeed, the kingdom of God is within you." (Luke 17:21) Do we believe the words of Jesus or not? If the kingdom is within us, we have access to all, and you are not limited by dollars or lack of dollars. I am not talking about doing foolish things like writing hot checks and making stupid decisions in the name of Christ. I am talking about believing and watching God make a way where there is no way.

When it looked like there was no way for Lazarus to come back from the dead, Jesus first wept sorrowfully with his friends, but then he raised Lazarus. After raising him, Jesus said, "Did I not tell you that if you believe, you will see the glory of God?" (John 11:40) I would like to encourage you that no matter how far gone a situation may seem, no matter how dead your finances are, and no matter what obstacles have been placed before you, close your eyes and return to a moment in childhood where you had unlimited belief. If you cannot find that place of innocence and belief, ask God to restore it to your memory. May that gift of faith rise up within you, and may joy fill your heart as you see the obstacles as being tiny little bubbles under the weight of a magnificent Father who loves you and backs you up.

You and your spouse are not defined by your finances.
Your finances are not your identity.
Your finances are not who you are.
Monetary lack does not dictate the quality of your time together.
You have access to everything.
Nothing is impossible.
Your spouse is more important than money.

Chapter 8

Facing Loss

"Unity is not when you agree with someone else. Unity is when you are willing to lay your life down for someone else."
Bill

In marriage, there is no doubt that you will go through times of loss, whether it's the loss of a loved one, loss of finances, material goods, friendships, perhaps even reputation. How are couples to function together during times of loss? Grief may look different for each person, and how they process their grief may vary along the path. Traci calls this the "willingness to walk through the valley of the shadow of death with your spouse." Walk with me for a moment, through some of my own process:

...So then, God created liquid and light and land and life and gave it all color and glued it together with gravity. And man would step out upon the sand and feel the warmth of the sun and the taste of the wind and the sound of the sea and breathe deeply only to say, "Whoa." And man was silent, locked in an inaudible sigh at the knowledge that he was indeed absolutely and eternally loved.

The night before my Dad died, I felt strangely alone. A cold awareness of physical mortality made the artificially warm air in the room especially uncomfortable as the snow fell outside. Wind normally blowing across the eastern Dakota prairie, tonight it was quiet and still. A question formed in the recesses of my consciousness that I had suppressed until the stillness lifted its words from my heart to my lips, and I breathed a question into the silence. "God, where are you?" No voice answered back. Atheism perhaps has no greater foundation than suffering and loss, for these moments of deep heart-breaking pain make it seem as if an omniscient and omnipresent God is absent. To dwell upon that can leave the strongest disciple in a crushing crucible of questioning the very existence of both the love of God and the God of love.

> *I breathed a question into the silence. "God, where are you?" No voice answered back.*

The question dissipated into the stillness, and suddenly there was a buzz as the screen of my phone lit up the room. Startled by the vibration on the table, I looked down to see who it was and I saw a picture of my wife. She was back home with our kids, but in that moment, the distance didn't matter. Her voice broke into my isolation and brought peace in the solitude. As I recounted the events of the day, she sat quietly at times, spoke softly at others, prayed with me, and the words she used gave a deep comfort. There's a difference between feeling forsaken and being forsaken. When we feel forsaken by God, sometimes the peace of Heaven can be heard in the voice of a trusted companion. In this case, I found the presence of God in the comfort of a person. In a world that exalts autonomy, God reveals Himself in the voice of a lover, the face of a friend, the kindness of a stranger. In creating humanity in His image and likeness, an infinite God has done the impossible and magnified Himself in His own creation. King

David, in Psalm 139, declared that there is nowhere that God cannot be found and nowhere we can go to flee from His presence. He cannot be absent, but He can be ignored. When we ignore the beauty of His reflection in others, we find it difficult to let Him shine within ourselves. Traci and I were one that night, for I heard the compassion of God in her sound. Compassion, however, doesn't erase suffering. It is the place where we find God present in the midst of loss. So then, suffering doesn't mean we are alienated from God.

The presence of God in our pain doesn't mean that pain and suffering are good. I will say without a doubt that suffering is evil. Much of it has no sensible point or rational purpose: young soldiers' lives who ended on a battlefield far from home, the persecution of hatred simply because of your skin, poverty and hunger in a world of wealth, or the abusive fist of a spouse who swore to cherish your heart. No wonder these moments void of compassion certainly do make it seem as though God is absent. Have you been there? I don't believe that God causes suffering. But neither does he erase it. If God were to eliminate the possibility of pain and suffering in the world, what good would our compassion be? Compassion in pain issues an invitation to transform, and it imparts divinity into our humanity. Compassion dignifies both the existence of the giver and receiver as validated, and shatters the bonds of slavery to simply being a victim who has lost control of the world.

Mercy can only be received when we come to the conclusion that we are no longer in control. The mercy of God is not merely found in the forgiveness of sin. The mercy of God is found when sacrificial compassion enters our moments of pain. Sacrificial compassion is not a means to exert power, but to exalt God. If
70

compassion edifies the ego, it serves no divine good, but when it magnifies Christ, our oneness in Him is revealed, and that revelation becomes our sanctuary. The compassion of God itself is our victory over the pain in this life. This is what it means to be perfected in unity. These are the words Christ prayed in John 17, that we would be perfected in unity. So then, unity has become the quest of marriage. But how we define unity is the foundation of our quest, and when the foundation is wrong, the quest is futile. If you believe that unity is agreement, then you have embarked on the quest of the religious. When people believe that unity is defined as agreement, they may go to great and destructive lengths to produce it. We may work to compose a better opinion for an intellectual wrestling match and humiliate our opponent into submission. We may attend classes to learn how to invite someone to pray a prayer that we made up to create a convert to our belief, and yet give no energy to making disciples who are filled with the sacrificial compassion of Christ. We may even label another as an "infidel" or "pagan" and see them as an enemy to be destroyed if they won't unite.

> *Mercy can only be received when we come to the conclusion that we are no longer in control.*

In marriage, we may get into endless arguments, hurling opinions like punches meant to knock some sense into our covenant partner. But unity is not agreement. Unity is not when you agree with someone else. Unity is when you are willing to lay down your life for someone else. This is the Christlike compassion that laid down His life for a world in complete disagreement with Him, and there, on the cross, He reconciled us back to unity with God. Now He has commissioned all of us with the ministry of reconciliation. Can you lay down your life for someone who doesn't agree with you? It's that sacrificial compassion that displays the kindness that leads to repentance or a change of heart and mind.

I buried my father a few days later, and Traci was by my side. We wept together, laughed together, and stood together in the snow to lay my father to rest. Covenant marriage means you lay down your life for another. When she stood at the altar on our wedding day, she was giving her life to be the one to walk with me through these moments of both joy and pain that touch, define, and unite us all. This mutual surrender to radical sacrificial compassion is the true love that reveals God to a hurting world, and answers the prayer of Jesus that we be perfected in unity.

"It's a strange feeling to watch your spouse experience loss."
Traci

Over the course of three decades of marriage, Bill and I have watched each other face various losses and disappointments. Whether it's losing friends and family, jobs, opportunities, or facing other disappointments, these are times to allow our love to increase. People grieve differently. What happens when the one we love hits a hard spot? How can we help them through it?

- *Keep communication open.*
- *Allow them to grieve.*
- *Reassure them of your presence and care.*
- *Ask how you can help.*

- Listen carefully.
- Offer support without critiquing or judging their response to the loss.
- Don't be afraid to reminisce and recall cherished moments with a loved one who has passed away.
- Encourage them without "Here's what you need to do." Encouragement shouldn't be a command or instruction.
- Pray.
- Remember to practice sacrificial compassion.

On the topic of prayer, I've found that when Bill and I pray together, something powerful happens. Love is experienced on a deeper level as our souls come together to communicate with God. But believe it or not, we usually have to make a conscious effort to pray together. I personally communicate with God all day long, and in the night. I wake up talking with Him and I fall asleep talking with Him. I know that Bill does the same. It's a continual conversation that's threaded throughout the course of everything we do. We sometimes forget to come together and talk with God as a couple. It can feel awkward at first, but then it becomes natural. We enjoy asking God to speak to us, and it's a lot of fun when you actually begin to hear or sense the same thing. It's a wonderful feeling to connect with your spouse on a spiritual level; it's like a stamp of approval or validation of your connection. Hearing God's "yes" over your union is uplifting on every level. It's in this place where we are reminded of our beautiful union with Him and with each other.

As Bill said before, unity is when you are willing to lay down your life for someone else, even if they don't agree with you. So, whether it is a season of grieving, triumph, joy, defeat, sickness or health, we can walk with our spouse in unity. Each season can help us to discover and explore a new facet of the one we love; to see a new angle, to experience an unfolding mystery, and be there to cheer them on into their next chapter. "Perfect love casts out fear." May we discover that perfect love, even when facing loss.

Chapter 9

The Journey Out of Bitterville

"He is perfect love that transcends the worst of evils."
Traci

Bitterness is a poison that robs us on every level. If we allow it to take root, it seeps into all of our relationships whether we realize it or not. Eventually, it comes out, even toward those we love. In many cases, one finds their passion, mission, or their life message in the very place where their heart, mind and soul were challenged. Sometimes the enemy lunges at our throats through people and things that we consider to be safe; even through our spouses at times. My observations and experiences have led me to a conclusion.

If we carry bitterness and resentment toward someone who has caused us pain, it is as if we are unknowingly feeding and empowering that very spirit that sought our destruction, to take form in such a way that we will not recognize it when it returns to deceive and devour us. Let me put it in easier terms. If the thing that hurt us, but did not destroy us, causes us to live in bitterness, it will return in another form to take that final blow to bring us down. Our own bitterness and resentment will cause us to walk ourselves to the threshold of destruction. One tiny wind can push us right over the edge. Perhaps that is why we are told "do not judge, so that you will not be judged."

When we carry unforgiveness, it is ultimately because of fear. For the offended, that statement is offensive. I know, because it once offended me, and it took some time for God to chip away at my hardness and the wall of protection I had placed around my heart. As anger and bitterness slipped away, little by little, my clarity and vision was restored. Fear, selfishness and unbelief will eventually lead us into the very prison that the assaulting spirit originally attempted to throw us into. Rather than pick up our sniper rifles, we should surrender ourselves to the fact that Jesus' blood is strong enough to take care of every offense and that He is perfect love

> *When we carry unforgiveness, it is ultimately out of fear.*

that transcends the worst of evils. As tempting as it may be to retaliate or seek revenge, I have learned to pray, "Create in me a clean heart. Renew a right spirit within me, that I might not be led to destruction." May we all live in such a way that Jesus gets everything He gave His life for. May we live in such a way that our marriage reflects the beauty of a life flowing from pure waters, untainted by bitterness. Where love is present, we see clearly. Where bitterness is present, our vision grows distorted and we lose discernment. Seeing our spouse through the eyes of love is the only way to grow together in unity.

Knowing Bill at the age of five is a huge benefit to me because when our marriage suffered on the rocks of disappointment, I was able to look into those big brown eyes and flashback to the little boy whom I played with in innocence and purity. There is something powerful about seeing your spouse as a child. We often forget that Jesus said, "Truly I say to you, unless you change and become like children, you will not enter the kingdom of heaven." Unless we become like children, we cannot see the Kingdom of Heaven. If we cannot see the child in our spouse, we are missing something of value. This goes back to the question of who they really are and who they are becoming. What did God imagine for that little child, the one who grew up, the one whom you chose to love? If we can push past the things of adulthood and journey back to the place of innocence, perhaps we can see something that will remind us of who they are becoming.

In seeing who our spouse is becoming, from God's perspective, we can navigate the temporal mistakes and attitudes of the moment. Maybe it seems impossible to see your spouse as ever having any innocence. Ask the Father to give you insight, a dream, or a vision about what He thought of when He created them. If you feel that you get a glimpse of your spouse in innocence, write it down! Hold onto that picture and speak that life over them. When they act in a way that's contrary to what you see, ask the Holy Spirit for wisdom in redirecting their soul toward goodness. It's worth a shot! And again, in regards to abusive situations, you are not required to play the savior and stay in detrimental conditions. You can exercise this search for innocence and original design from afar, even without having any form of contact with the person. The things of the spirit are powerful and effective; one only needs to be open to it in order to see change.

"Let all bitterness and wrath and anger and clamor and slander be put away from you, along with all malice. Be kind to one another, tender-hearted, forgiving each other, just as God in Christ also has forgiven you." ~ Ephesians 4:31-32

When we didn't deserve forgiveness, Christ erased our record of wrongs. Are we supposed to do the same for others? For our spouse?

"For if you forgive other people when they sin against you, your heavenly Father will also forgive you. But if you do not forgive others their sins, your Father will not forgive your sins." ~ Matthew 6:14-15

Wow! That sounds harsh, doesn't it? If we do not forgive, we will not be forgiven. To forgive is to release someone from your judgment. In doing so, you free yourself from judgment and release yourself from a prison of turmoil. "But they don't deserve my forgiveness. They must pay!"

"The Lord our God is merciful and forgiving, even though we have rebelled against him." ~ Daniel 9:9

"So watch yourselves. If your brother sins, rebuke him, and if he repents, forgive him. If he sins against you seven times in a day, and seven times comes back to you and says, 'I repent,' forgive him." ~ Luke 17:3-4

"Love is patient, love is kind. It does not envy, it does not boast, it is not proud. It does not dishonor others, it is not self-seeking, it is not easily angered, it keeps no record of wrongs. Love does not delight in evil but rejoices with the truth." ~ 1 Corinthians 13:4-6

If it offends us that the Father forgives what we cannot, then in essence, we are jealous or envious of what our offender has been given. According to Proverbs 14:30, jealousy and envy are rottenness to the bones. Like a cancer, it will eat you up. In marriage, you will be presented with many opportunities to choose bitterness and resentment, or grace and forgiveness. Marriage is an opportunity for transformation, at times forged in the fire, and sealed with the kiss of the Covenant Keeper who brought us to life with His very breath.

The breath of God. Adam came to life in a face-to-face encounter with a loving Father, infused with His very breath. Later on, in John 20:22, Jesus breathed on the disciples, saying, "Receive the Holy Spirit." Think about the power of a kiss. Why do people enjoy kissing? What provokes humans to touch their lips to another person's lips and linger there? I believe it has to do with shared breath, shared life; an infusion of one into the other. It is a deep, intimate place in which we were birthed from the start. We were created for unhindered intimacy where bitterness cannot remain. When you kiss your spouse, let it be a life-giving experience in which you release peace and newness to them. It can be a fresh start, wiping the slate clean, and choosing that "70 times 7" forgiveness once again.

For a thorough journey into the mysteries and power of grace to heal you and your spouse, I highly encourage you to read Bill's book, Reckless Grace. Co-written with our dear friend, Brit Eaton, the male and female perspective of grace is well covered and deeply explored in Scripture. They offer excellent, practical ways to apply grace to any relationship, and find freedom from the prison of bitterness.

Chapter 10

The Reckless, Raging Fury

"...we wove that into the fabric of our marriage. And it saved us."
Traci

In 1997, Bill and I had the privilege of building a new relationship with a most unique and beautiful man named Rich Mullins. Rich was a very popular contemporary Christian songwriter, singer, and musician who made a notable impact on the world. Instead of being consumed with his success, he decided to move to the Navajo Nation to teach music to the children on the reservation. Rich could have lived a life of wealth, but he chose a life of humble simplicity. I'll never forget the first time I saw him in concert. I wondered who the guy was that nonchalantly walked out on the stage with bare feet, torn jeans and a white T-shirt. When he picked up the mic and began talking and playing music, I then realized he was "the Rich Mullins!" I had never seen anyone like him. Gentleness, rawness, and a genuine mark of Christ rested on him.

The stunning words that he penned in The Love of God, paints a beautiful picture of God's grace:

"There's a wideness in God's mercy

I cannot find in my own
And He keeps His fire burning
To melt this heart of stone
Keeps me aching with a yearning
Keeps me glad to have been caught
In the reckless raging fury
That they call the love of God

Now I've seen no band of angels
But I've heard the soldiers' songs
Love hangs over them like a banner
Love within them leads them on
To the battle on the journey
And it's never gonna stop
Ever widening their mercies
And the fury of His love

Oh the love of God
And oh the love of God
The love of God

Joy and sorrow are this ocean
And in their every ebb and flow
Now the Lord a door has opened
That all Hell could never close
Here I'm tested and made worthy
Tossed about but lifted up
In the reckless raging fury
That they call the love of God"

Let's talk about how these words apply to couples. As I encounter people each day and hear their stories, I notice two things. There are the once-defiled who know they have been made clean and whole, and there are the clean and whole who do not realize that they are no longer defiled. The experience of grace produces the first, and the experience of judgment creates the latter. It is easy to recognize those who have known the reckless, raging fury known as the love of God. There is a sound, a light, a love, and humility that's evident in their countenance.

I marvel at this phrase found in 1 Corinthians 6:9-11: "And that is what some of you were." (NIV) "And such were some of you." (KJV) The apostle Paul reveals that who you once were is not who you truly are.

"Or do you not know that wrongdoers will not inherit the kingdom of God? Do not be deceived: Neither the sexually immoral nor idolaters nor adulterers nor men who have sex with men nor thieves nor the greedy nor drunkards nor slanderers nor swindlers will inherit the kingdom of God. And that is what some of you **were. But** you were washed, you were sanctified, you were justified in the name of the Lord Jesus Christ and by the Spirit of our God."

I have met far too many Christians who still do not know just how clean they have been made, so they continue living a life in which they fall prey to sin, walking in a false identity that they were never created for. They strive to live by the letter of the law rather than by the heart and life of God's Spirit. This striving keeps them locked in chains. We have often focused on the "will not inherit the Kingdom of God" part and miss the "were" and the "but" that God so gladly gave His Son for. If Jesus came to

Who you once were is not who you truly are.

82

set captives and prisoners free, then who are we to keep ourselves and each other locked in chains? And who are we to keep others locked in the chains of our judgments and expectations?

If Jesus could look down from the cross upon the men who beat Him, spit on Him and ripped apart His flesh, and declare these words over them with a heart of compassion: "Father, forgive them, for they know not what they do," then who are we to withhold forgiveness? Everyone should have the opportunity to know the love and grace that Rich Mullins describes as a reckless, raging fury. Grace, furious? You would understand that phrase if you have ever been redeemed from the hand of the enemy, out of a life of destruction.

As for myself, I have gone from being both a prisoner and a captive. A prisoner is one who is held in prison because of something they did wrong. A captive is held in prison because of something someone else did. I, Traci, admit that I still have a vigilante side of me that wants the kind of justice that satisfies the bit of my heart that I must purposely and daily surrender. That's why I studied Krav Maga many years ago. There is a certain satisfaction I once found in hand-to-hand combat, but I learned that unforgiveness and bitterness immobilizes who I really am, and it prevents me from living the life I am meant to live. There are times when I want to "pull out the guns" and then I think for a moment. Would I rather become internally scarred and dead to God's heart, or would I rather lay down in the fields of gold that I have known as 'grace?' I choose the latter.

Rich's song taught me and Bill a lot about the grace of God, and those lessons impacted our marriage deeply. Each line of his songs were like a facet of God and of who we are called to be to one another. Each truth reminded us that we were born to display the image and likeness of God, and our marriage would be the first place we should put that grace and light on display. Imagine that, your marriage is like a lamp stand, a light on a hill, a beacon of hope for a broken world that's thirsty for love. For family. For a picture of union; genuine picture of being intertwined with the One who makes us whole and filled us with His breath.

Two weeks after Bill and I sat with Rich and his band at a restaurant in San Antonio, Texas, chatting into the wee hours of the morning while our children rested in the booth, Rich left this earth instantly in a terrible car accident. I couldn't believe it when I heard the news. Bill and I cried for several days. Later, we were surprised by a letter that showed up in our mailbox from someone who had stopped at the scene of the accident. "I found your name and address on a piece of paper that was thrown from Rich's car. I just wanted to know who you were. I figured it must have been important if he had your address written down." Yes, it was important. Rich was our first introduction to the reckless grace of God and we wove that into the fabric of our marriage. And it saved us.

Chapter 11

Sex and Covenant

"Shame will cause people to act out irrational behavior and call it holy."
Bill

It is not enough to think about love. Love must be experienced, fought for, tasted, and rested in. Love's force possesses you, mind and body. When you think of the deepest, most profound way to experience love on a physical level, you think of sex. I have been a sexual creature all my life, and so have you. If you have grown up in a repressed, conservative household, sex was likely never or rarely talked about. Is it strange that the most thought about subject on the human mind is never talked about, out of a warped definition of embarrassment disguised as respect?

The conservatism I grew up with tended to live within the confines of the lie that sexuality is a condition that we live with, and we treat it like a disease in our public conversation only to be enjoyed in our private moments. If we are as sick as our secrets, then the church is diseased with the covering up of the fact that even Christians are created to be sexual and to enjoy sex. After all, your genitals did not fall off or shut down when you accepted Jesus, did they? If you grew up in a Christian household, how was it for you as a young person? When you discovered that you enjoyed sexuality, did it feel bad or wrong? For many people, liking sexuality feels as warped to our religious consciousness as enjoying cancer. As shocking as that statement would be, ask yourself this question. Which would be easier to announce to people: that you love sex or that you have cancer? The truth is that for most people, they are both equally difficult statements to voice. A cancer announcement would generate sympathy, but a sex announcement would generate looks that display a betrayal of social norms that might look like disgust, but it would only be hiding an internally empathetic response from nearly every person in the room. Because the truth is that sexuality is pleasure created by God, and deep down inside, everyone knows this.

The purity and beauty of sexuality, like everything else, is defiled by expressions that involve lying and betrayal. William Shakespeare said, "Love all, trust few, wrong no one." To love everyone is the mandate of every person, but our giving of love does not automatically default to sexual expression. How you express love is effective only if it is perceived as love by the receiver, which is why people can have sex and there be no love or even intimacy involved, for within the context of modern human culture, sex is as much a way to experience pleasure as riding a roller coaster, or attending a concert, going to the movies, or getting a foot massage. For many people, it simply falls into the category of entertainment.

On one hand, when something so all encompassing as sexuality becomes no big deal, there is a loss of value in its purpose and less fulfillment in its mere existence. In other words, it becomes easy to ignore. For people who struggle with compulsive addictions to all things sexual, this seems like an impossibility. Talk to an adult industry professional however, and you'll quickly realize just how

86

desensitized a person can become. One revelation they do tend to understand, which is of great value, is that there is an intimacy found beyond the realm of human sexuality and that is the ultimate quest. For those who believe in it, it is commonly called "true love."

The hyper-sensitive and ultra-suppressive find sex both impossible to talk about casually, and ignore casually. In other words, sex freaks some people out and makes their Christian brain short circuit. Like the man who left a church because he stopped in at the gas station across the street and saw a box of condoms for sale. He claimed that seeing the condoms caused him to stumble so much that he could not even concentrate on the message and knew he could never go to a church that was near a gas station that sold such things. That is a true story. When people think that sex is the biggest deal of big deals that has ever been, the struggles with managing appetite and the rational and irrational weaknesses that overtake a person can produce inordinate amounts of shame and guilt. And if there is one thing that's a downer on sexual fulfillment and can kill your buzz quicker than anything, it is shame. Secrecy might seem sexy, but shame is most certainly not. Shame will cause people to act out irrational behavior and call it "holy."

Shame is religion's way of convincing you that you are evil because of what you have done, where the Holy Spirit is the Father's way of convincing you that you are righteous because of what Jesus has done. See, if I can convince you that you are out of favor with God, it puts you in a position where I can control your behavior by taking responsibility for your life. In the church, we call that accountability. And to justify controlling people who seemingly have no self-control, the church has preached some atrocious theology that generates a response motivated by guilt,

87

shame, and fear. And that is where I think Paul's liberating blanket statement of behavior applies so well.

"All things are lawful (permissible), not all things are beneficial (edifying)." Whatever your theological position on God's perspective of human sexuality, even the most liberal of persons for whom anything goes, would concede that not everything goes well. Anything that brings shame and pain to the heart and dulls our ability to detect and discern the voice and know the mind of God is of no benefit, and that is what qualifies as sin. For some people, it is an enlightened existence to, rather than change the behavior, simply become convinced that the behavior is fine and should not produce shame and guilt. But ask someone who is hurt or betrayed by your behavior and they would say that such selfish, recklessness is no enlightenment to any perspective. No, on this note, William Shakespeare had it right. Love all and do wrong to no one.

Love was never meant to betray, to cause pain, or justify lies. Might I offer this suggestion? Share your kindness liberally. Share your commitment carefully. Share your heart rarely. Share your love as liberally as you do your kindness. But give of your sexuality when all four (kindness, commitment, heart, and love) are present in you and presented to you. Ideally defined, a marriage ceremony is supposed to be the public profession that this moment is the convergence of all of these qualities.

The embrace of sexual intimacy is the prized expression of authentic love, and herein is a value and satisfaction far above a selfish, animalistic, physically dominating fulfillment. Genuine intimacy and true pleasure is found in the hand of God who is Love, and it is that hand upon your life and behavior that will illuminate the deepest revelation of you as a sexual creation of a very good God.

"Our beds should be a place of safety."
Traci

After more than two decades of standing in line at various grocery stores, I have become very familiar with the headlines of popular magazines. After reading the same types of headlines over and over again, I realized that these articles are merely being recreated in different forms in order to hook people. Sex sells. Marketers know this well, and that's why you see it everywhere. Some of those headlines read:

Mind Blowing Sex
The Greatest Sex
Deep Sex
78 Ways to Turn Him On
25 Tips From Guys
Be A Sex Genius
The Secret of Sex

On and on the list goes, and I have to wonder, after two decades of seeing the same headlines, have they actually figured it out yet? The truth is that sex can be really amazing and it does not take a genius to figure that out. It does, however, take a dedicated heart to become a person who commits to tune in to their spouse, learning what they like, how they feel, and knowing what moves them throughout the years of change. I feel that anyone who claims that sex gets dull after being with the same person for many years is just missing something, or they've become stuck in a routine, or accepted the common theme that it goes downhill over time. Before I go further, I do want to acknowledge that some people may experience problems due to health or past abuse, or other events that have interfered with a healthy sex life. In those cases, there is hope through the right counselors, therapists, prayer, and working together. Many people have been victims of sexual abuse, so a spouse should take the time to consider their partner's experience and help them through a healing process. Bill and I have known couples that overcame difficulty through therapy and found a fulfilling sex life after overcoming obstacles. Our beds should be a place of safety. There, healing can begin. When you are more concerned for the pleasure of your spouse than your own, you will ultimately find greater fulfillment.

Sex can become better, and even more frequent, with time. The ebbs and flows, the ups and downs of life are normal, however. There are seasons for everything, so don't freak out if you're just too tired to make it happen. Raising children, working jobs, and trying to meet daily expectations definitely put a damper on things at times. Couples often feel they have to meet the standard of a passionate, intense encounter much like we see on television or in the movies. But this is not always reality. Sure, those moments happen from time to time, but the truth is, when you're exhausted, but still wanting to connect with your spouse, lazy sex is okay. The effort to connect is honorable. And sometimes a good cuddle is the best intimacy for the moment. Stop trying to live up to a steamy shot produced by directors and actors with cuts, edits, filters, and "action."

I like to consider the beauty of a master musician who values and knows his beloved instrument well. Perhaps a violin or cello. There is a certain sound that he has become one with, and he knows exactly where to touch and how to touch to create a certain sound. Each instrument has its own unique "feel" and over time, it is as if the two become one. The musician is willing to learn, write and play new songs, pouring his passion and creativity into his instrument. Depending on the musician's feelings, he may play notes of joy, sadness, silliness, or dramatic tones. No matter which feelings are underlying in the moment, he's still creating, touching, and maintaining connection with his instrument through which he expresses himself. He knows exactly how to bring pleasure. If we treat our spouse better than the things we've come to cherish and spend our time on, we will find ourselves pleasantly surprised by the level of pleasure that's been there all along. After almost thirty years of marriage, we've found this to be true. The music of the season, the method of the moment; all of it matters. And you may be surprised to find things improving with time. The ups and downs of life can make intimate moments so much sweeter.

Aside from talking about the physical aspect of marriage, I'm reminded of our early years of ministry, and how we often met with couples for their "pre-marital counseling." One of the first things we would do is have them list their expectations of each other, even down to who would take out the trash. We figured that being aware of those expectations would help the couple succeed in fulfilling each other. Today, we cringe a bit at the thought. What we should have done was take the lists and rip them to shreds. The truth is that it is impossible for any human to meet every single expectation of another, and continue doing so year after year. There is something deeper than expectation. There is a mysterious union in covenant that is insanely beautiful and few really learn to see it. Those who dare to walk with another through sickness, difficulties, disappointments, and shakings of all kinds are usually the ones that get to discover deeper facets of union that actually enhance love and intimacy. My questions for those considering marriage are:

1. Are you willing to walk with this person through their "dark night of the soul?"

2. Are you willing to lay down your expectations, allowing this person room to grow and become who they are?

3. Are you willing to pay close attention to the heart of the one you love? Study, observe, and pursue that heart?

4. What if this person hurts your heart? Do you love them enough to love them through it, until they learn to love more?

5. Are you willing to explore your partner's feelings and desires, setting their needs above your own while remaining faithful?

If the answer is "yes," then chances are that you will get to experience the amazing intimacy and power of love. And wrapped into the mix is the blessing of great sex!

Chapter 12

The Lover's Job

"True love is magnified by honesty and acceptance."
Bill

When God made you, He did so in Love. Everything about who you truly are, originated in Love Himself. His Spirit was breathed into the costume you wear with great affection. And it is this Love that defines you, reveals Him, and unveils the boundless horizon of His goodness. You have been designed with a blueprint that originated in the mind of God. You are in the most literal sense, a manifestation of God's imagination. You are the daydream of Love Himself.

Now you have one job in this life. To be loved. To be loved with outrageous abandon. Heaven has conspired to love you. Eternity has constructed an existence where love shines without inhibition. Do you think that you are supposed to love? That you are supposed to love the best you can in this life? Do you love well? Do you justify loving poorly when you cannot seem to generate enough affection for people? Does the idea of loving seem like work and before you know it, the end of the thought leaves you too tired to even begin the effort? To you, I say you are not doing your job.

Remember? Your job is to be loved. God is trying to communicate to you something vital to understanding. It is next to impossible to love beyond the revelation of how loved you are. You cannot generate love for another on your own. Love is a gift that is born of God, and to love apart from that gift is a religious action that is born of a simple desire to please another person. Love, duty, and the fear of man all motivate people to kindness, and the actions are very much the same. But duty and fear will both wear you out, because you are the fuel for their fire, and when you are the fuel, you will burn out.

Love is energizing, invigorating, and supernatural in its ability to infuse you with life and strength in the midst of supernatural effort. Ask God to reveal His love for you and to you, without creating the box of expectation, and position yourself to receive the grace that He has prepared for you from before the foundation of the world. From that place, you will love with far greater effect than you could ever imagine.

Every relationship is an opportunity to be a character in a play, and for those who have control issues, they take the director's chair. Maybe not with conscious intent, but they just cannot help but predict the next series of events, sentences, words. If you are the director type, you probably do not even realize that there are people out there who do not think the way you do. Or maybe it's because you know there are people who will not take charge that you start calling the shots.

Relational directors have a hard time with the cast members who will not cooperate. The lines are annoying, the blocking is all wrong, and the whole plot line of the relationship gets thrown off. Strip all of this control away and bring it down to simply absorbing and processing the story of another. If you are invited into it, then offer what you may. But the question is, can you love a character that you cannot direct? Can you embrace a person you did not create? On the other side, we will call this person the supporting player. They look to the directors to find out who they are supposed to be, but by themselves they may be something totally different. They are not weaker, and may even look down on someone's need to control and simply go along with it, like an adult condescends to a child's imagination to sip tea out of empty miniature teacups and be called a different name altogether.

Giving in does not hurt and, in fact, makes the relationship amusing. In their own way, the director and the supporting player work with each other to produce their relational story. When it stops working, the story ends. Authentic love lets another person's character develop unhindered and fully accepted. It finds the fascination in the organic spirit and sees the beauty in the scarred soul. It can see you at your brightest moment of heroism and your darkest moment of vulnerability and loves you still.

When you are seen for who you are, and accepted anyway, that is love's expression. If you cannot be known, you will not be loved. Love may be given, but to your character, not to you, and it will always remain just out of your heart's reach. True love is magnified by honesty and acceptance. Magnified beyond words. True love will leave you speechless, breathless, wide-eyed in wonder at the tenderness with which it embraces your overworked heart and leaves it at peace. There are no walls in love's theater. True love gives up the right to yell, "Cut!!" and allows the cameras to keep rolling, even when the

> *Love is the ultimate force of empowerment.*

script is not perfect, even when the props are not in place, even when the budget is not there, when the reviews are lousy, when the love scenes are awkward, when the music is wrong, when the lighting is off, when the cues and timing are poor, none of it matters. Love always sees a masterpiece.

There is no weakness that cannot be erased by being loved. It is the ultimate force of empowerment and motivated by the knowledge that you are loved. There is literally nothing that seems impossible. Consequently, when you return that love, fear completely evaporates under its molten intensity. It is a relational cycle of superhuman acceleration that sees a mountainous obstacle to be as unthreatening as a house of cards, and shakes the earth beneath your every step as if the entire universe is in awe at the spectacle of your fearless courage.

I have wondered at 1 John 4:7-8:

"Beloved, let us love one another. For love is of God and everyone that loves is born of God and knows God. He that does not love, does not know God, for God is love."

I believe the key to every good and perfect thing in this life and eternity is hidden behind the revelation of how loved we are by Love Himself. To the extent that you realize you are loved, you are empowered to love, equipped with strength, and in loving, you are filled with the courage of heaven. We are designed to be an expression of the Love of the Father to one another. It is as if God is embracing one person through another. No doubt God loves in and of Himself, apart from us, but He is not apart from us. And that understanding of union equips us to love beyond what we thought we were ever capable of, but inwardly wished we were. And you are capable. Your ability to Love is not tied to your personality, your training, your upbringing, your past, or your present. Your Love is in surrender to the Holy Spirit of God to simply do what He does through you. The Lover's job is a privilege in which you and your spouse are the recipients.

Chapter 13

Feeling Off-Kilter

"And someone who loves you and is not in agreement
with you, is not your enemy."
Bill

I have found that one of the vulnerabilities of loving is that you have just grafted the artery through which your happiness flows into another person and now you both contribute to the collective happiness of one another to fullness of life, or cut it off to the depression of both. Either way, you have just become conjoined twins united at the heart, and though you may retain individual interests and personalities, when one is not happy, the other is not either. I do not think this is a design flaw or a problem to overcome. I believe this is a testimony to our union with God and one another.

When I do not believe God is happy, I reflect that condition toward this world. We reflect the perceived mood of the object of our affection. If I look at my wife and she is looking at something with an angry look, without even realizing it, I mirror the same look in the same direction. As if I am displaying my distaste for whatever is causing her normally beautiful smile to scowl. We display our love and demonstrate our union for another by taking their mood or the emotional overflow of the condition of the heart, and exaggerating it, just to make sure they know that we empathize. If they are sitting there happy, we get up and dance. If they are angry, we look for someone to fight. We mirror them and raise the stakes. How does someone else affect you like that? Because you are joined in heart.

Sometimes love will see the heart of the lover going to a place that will cause damage, and in that moment, love is demonstrated in conflict. That is, someone you love disagrees with you. Disagreement is not always a lack of love. Sometimes it is an act of love. And someone who loves you and is not in agreement with you is not your enemy. As a matter of fact, they may save your life, for in standing against your will to self-destruct, they are actually saving themselves too. Let them. After all, you are sharing one heart.

How do you give and receive love when things seem off-kilter? Though everyone both gives and receives, people sway to emphasize a lifestyle of one over the other. And you can see it in the eyes. Why the eyes? When you have something to give, your eyes show it, and when you have something you need, your eyes reveal it. When a giver and a receiver lock eyes, there is an unspoken demand that is initiated. Receivers do not often lock eyes with each other because they cannot see past themselves. Givers do not often lock eyes with each other because they have difficulty receiving. This is probably why opposites end up attracting and also why marriage therapy is a huge business.

> *When I do not believe God is happy, I reflect that condition toward this world.*

It is not very often that you find two givers and two receivers falling in love, but they should. When you see that you have what another lacks, you find what appears to be a fit. But it only exists in the context of recognizing the lack in someone else, and pretty soon their weakness and lack of appreciation for what you have produces conflict, where all of the books tell you ought to be a complimentary fit. What I'm trying to say is that opposites do attract, to the inherent need to fix each other. The truth

> *As long as there is union there is life.*

is we fix ourselves in the very exchange of love. As long as love is passed back and forth, there is relationship, and as long as there is union, there is life. For if the one you love and the one who loves you happen to be the same person, you are in a most rare and fortunate position.

"There is a depth to grace that may take a lifetime to discover."
Traci

There was a time in our marriage where everything seemed off-kilter. Bill and I seemed to be on opposite ends of the earth, a great chasm between us. I felt lost and I didn't know how to reach him. There will be times in relationships when this happens, but don't panic. It's a time to learn and a time to see the faithfulness of God in the midst of our own human conditions that make love appear to be a lie. During that season, I felt like I was climbing a mountain called Grace. Many times, I became weary of giving grace, trust and love because it sometimes disappointed. I would find myself in a good, seemingly safe place on the side of the mountain, but the pinnacle seemed out of reach. Disappointment and pain would come and I would find myself spiraling down into a deep pit of

100

insecurity, anger and sadness. Why did joy seem to escape me? Joy and grace were like precious jewels locked away behind numerous locks and barriers. I would capture glimpses of its brilliant light, but I could not touch or feel it. I became weary of the climb, but more importantly, I became weary of the pit. Would I press through and reach the pinnacle of grace? Did I actually have it within me to continue loving and believing the best? Would I let my fears and insecurities keep me from peering over the mountaintop, frightened of what may be on the other side?

> *Don't allow the "off" times to cause you to think that you're headed for destruction.*

When I finally gave my pain, doubts, and fears to God and asked for His heart and thoughts, I became saturated with His presence. I no longer asked Him to come into my heart. Instead, I asked that He take me into His heart. I found unbelievable, indescribable joy. I made it to the peak and the view was magnificent, yet I knew there was more. There is a depth to grace that may take a lifetime to discover. The little bit that I have already experienced convinces me that God's love is real and penetrating. It was in that place, at the pinnacle, that I was able to see clearly, and Bill was not as far away as I thought. In reality, we were closer than ever before. Because of the love of God who carried us in our own darkness, we were kept and preserved when everything was off-kilter. Don't allow the "off" times to cause you to think that you're headed for destruction. I believe that every season we experience in our marriages is a valuable time for learning to love, even when love feels a bit out of reach.

"It is possible to fall in love with the same person more than once in a lifetime."
Bill

When I was younger, I made flippant promises. They were not promises that I intended to break, nor were they promises I did not care about. Rather, I like a challenge. A promise was a self-imposed assignment that, if completed well, would result in the happiness of another and the increase of reputation. So I challenged myself with the phrase, "I promise..." Far more daunting was the wishful command in the form of a question, "Do you promise?" Either way, it was a game to be won, unless it is lost, then it is no longer a game.

Being married at the age of eighteen puts our now almost three-decade marriage in a rare bracket of those who have made it this far despite having started so young. We were young enough to have undergone quite a few personality changes over the years and through the evolution of likes and dislikes, I have learned something quite valuable. I learned that it is possible to fall in love with the same person more than once in a lifetime. If you are unwilling to do that, then one day when they wake up and are not the person you married, you will find a way to justify breaking the promise. Promises are not meant to be the bars that imprison us within the confines of a miserable existence of our own construction. They are made in moments when we realize that this thing that is being promised is very important. A promise says that "this important moment needs to be remembered." Promises are reminders that, at one time or another, this thing that was promised was important enough to warrant the use of the word in the first place. When you forget its importance, you can still remember

102

your promise. And rather than be angry at the promise, maybe take a minute to remember the moment in which the promise was made, and know once again why it was so important.

If that which was important then is still important now, keep the promise and rejoice at the reality that there was something in your life important enough to call for a promise to be made in the first place. Those moments are a gift worth treasuring.

To fall in love is often to find someone who is the answer to our questions.

Who am I supposed to be with?

Who will love me?

And we ask them questions that we ask about ourselves.

Why do you love me?

What about me is there to love?

What made you love me in the first place?

They are all the same question really, just in different versions. We ask questions about them, too, mostly to answer questions about ourselves.

So where did you come from?

What are your beliefs about .....?

What music do you like?

We are just really asking another question about ourselves.

Is this person comparable and compatible with me?

Making another person the answer to your endless litany of questions about yourself is an unhealthy way of trying to find yourself in another person. I do not want to imply that asking questions is a bad thing, because it is not. But I think a simple shift in perspective can clear up quite a bit of confusion. Live with the other person being the question to which you are the answer. This requires listening, learning, and loving, and in the process of becoming the answer to their ever changing and endlessly challenging questions, you may discover who you really are in the process. Or at least be aware of who you really are becoming. Remembering this can keep us in a place of peace when everything seems off-kilter. Treasure the promise and embrace the truth that it is possible to fall in love with your spouse again. Instead of panicking over the how and when, rest in the grace of God, walk in love, and watch how the story unfolds.

Chapter 14

The Power of Covenant

"When our 'love' fails, the Covenant Keeper's does not."
Traci

When you don't feel strong enough to keep up your "end of the deal" or your part of the covenant that you made, you can rest in God's ability to keep covenant. When you realize Christ is in you, then you can rest in the fact that the Covenant Keeper is within you it is Him who empowers you to keep your promises. When the covenant seems ruined, we often give up the hope of redemption, but the fact is that the Christ's blood is enough to wipe the slate clean. Things may not be the same, but He can make them better than before.

Let's explore a key found in the covenant between David and Jonathan (1 Samuel chapters 18 and 20). In studying covenant, David and Jonathan's relationship is certainly one to explore. Why would someone of royal status desire to exchange their clothing with a poor shepherd and commit their life, loyalty, and support to them? This is a true story, a true moment in history that's powerfully inspiring. The beauty of the story is this: When Jonathan, the son of a king, watched as a mere shepherd boy conquered a giant that everyone feared, Jonathan was intrigued and drawn to the anointing of God upon David's life. The presence of God was evident.

In 1 Samuel 18, Jonathan gave his own robe to David, along with his sword, bow and his belt. Imagine a warrior prince giving these valued possessions, and his very identity to a shepherd boy. That is exactly what Jesus did for us when He allowed man to draw out His blood and tear His flesh. He was making covenant with us, stripping Himself of His robe of righteousness and taking upon Himself our shame, clothing us in His righteousness and making us priests and kings, a royal priesthood. Jonathan's belt represents strength. Jesus traded us His strength for our weakness. He gave us His sword, His "weapons," in essence, taking upon Himself our own enemies. And, interestingly, he teaches

> *Jesus traded us His strength for our weakness.*

us to bless and pray for our enemies. We are in covenant. And through grace, and His invitation to man to be in union with Him, He has imparted the ability to turn adversaries into advocates.

Why would a King be drawn to make covenant with people like us? He sees what we carry, the seed that He placed within us. He breathed life into us and predestined us to be carriers of His glory. To allow us to remain apart from Him and live a life less than what He created us for is against His nature. I believe that is why He was compelled to come to Earth. The most amazing part is that He keeps His covenant with us. Humans have extremely high expectations when it comes to promises, but God has been merciful to us beyond what we deserve, as He continually forgives when we fail to meet His "expectations." He is patient enough and loving enough to forgive us and love us into our destiny. Covenant is stronger than we realize. The power of the blood of Jesus lies far beyond our ability to comprehend. Ask Him about His covenant with you and let Him reveal how you have been clothed in His righteousness, prepared for battle and wrapped in His arms. Your life may not be perfect, but it can become more beautiful than you have ever imagined.

Now consider the covenant you made with your spouse. How does it even compare to the covenant of our Creator? If we strip away our selfishness, our perceived needs, and our own pleasure as Christ did, then we just might see that marriage is not about our personal pleasure. Even though, I find marriage to be incredibly pleasurable, it has taken work at times to get there. Pleasure is part of our inheritance, but there's a power in finding it through the laying down of self. In looking at the example of Christ and Jonathan, have you stripped yourself of your status, riches, strength, and power, only to willfully and happily hand it over to your spouse, the one with whom you made covenant? Do you care more for their life than you do your own? Would you lay down your life for them? I think many of us feel we would or have, but what happens in the moments when you feel you can't keep covenant? Turn to the Covenant Keeper. Lean into His heart. If your covenant is broken, He has the power to keep it. You've heard the verse that says "a threefold cord is not easily broken." Perhaps you and your spouse don't feel strong enough to pull through, but that third "cord," the Father, Son, and Holy Spirit, within whom you are included, are powerful enough to keep covenant. When our "love" fails, the Covenant Keeper's does not. Love never fails.

When the trials of life shake you to the core and you begin to feel separate from God, remember what Jesus said in John 14:20. "On that day you will know that I am in My Father, and you are in Me, and I in you." Imagine that. You are in Him and He is in you, and

He is in the Father. You are one with the Covenant Keeper, and that's enough to cause you to refuse the lies and accusations of an enemy who wants to destroy covenant. Rest in your union with Christ. You are not your own. You were bought with a price, and He will see you through.

And we have known and believed the love that God has for us. God is love, and he who abides in love abides in God, and God in him.
1 John 4:16

There is no fear in love; but perfect love casts out fear, because fear involves torment. But he who fears has not been made perfect in love.
1 John 4:18

But why can't we seem to get this covenant thing down?

> *Covenant always wins.*

I have watched many who are close to me wear the pain of betrayal on their faces; their bodies bear the death of a covenant. Smiles have weakened. Eyes once filled with joy, struggle to lift their lids long enough to dare to greet another day. Do they dare to love again? My husband has taught me, "Covenant always wins." Even though it doesn't seem like it in this world, I do believe it's true. As I have scoured through many books of the Bible, like Hosea, Amos, Jeremiah, and many others, I see the pain in God's heart as He watches those He loves staggering in a cesspool of what they believe to be love. It is called deception. Yet, the Lover stands by, sometimes feeling the desire to destroy the very ones that He longed for in the beginning, yet His heart moves from anger to love. I believe the anger is only toward that which is an obstacle to love. Yet He forgives. He continues to love. He gives and pursues. Are we capable of that kind of love?

There have been moments when I feared loving. If you never want to hurt, then by all means, avoid relationship. However, in doing so, you forfeit the treasure of truly living; living deeply and living fully, and that would be the greatest pain of all. Living a life in which you never moved the heart of another, brought life to a soul, or allowed someone else to move your heart, that would be a tragedy. That's an emptiness that far outweighs the pain of loving. Sometimes, the barrier to love is totally based on misperception, miscommunication and misunderstanding, which means that the barrier is based on lies. The barrier is merely an illusion. The only power the enemy truly has is his lies. The lie holds no power until we choose to believe it, therefore, we are the ones who empower a lie and set it on course to bring destruction. Once a lie is believed, we have opened the door to the influence of darkness, and once we stick our foot in the door, we usually become convinced that there is no turning back, and that we might just stumble upon something we have longed for if we will continue justifying the lie.

A fog enters our mind, and slowly, or sometimes suddenly, we are convinced that our mess is actually destiny. How deluded we become as we begin listening to the voice of hell itself. It's as if we pause just long enough to take a glance, thinking that perhaps what we once thought was love may have actually been a farce, so we move into a trap, believing we will be set free. So, what of misperception? What of miscommunication? Sometimes a lack of communication is the culprit. In my case, my husband and I once uncovered a slightly hilarious misperception in our own relationship. After almost nineteen years of marriage, we discovered that my face was the problem. I have a weak muscle on the left side of my face that causes my closed-lip smile to appear as a smirk, when viewed from the left. Since my husband is often the one who drives our vehicle while we are on the road, he could only see the left side of my face, seemingly smirking, while he shared a joke or funny thought. I was amused and enjoyed his thoughts, but from the appearance of my face, he interpreted my look as the presence of contempt. He decided that I must have thought he was a fool. Talk about sad. Thank God we discovered what was really happening! Now we can enjoy conversation and he knows that I'm not putting him down with my visage. Learn the face of your lover!

Is there anything interfering with your marriage covenant? Is there anything you dare not tell your spouse? If so, lay it all out on the table and cut off the ties that are interfering with true intimacy. A safe place is truly a safe place when there is, first, total honesty within covenant. A secret sin unconfessed becomes a stronghold. You are only as sick as your secrets. The enemy has a way of making that "secret place" feel safe, when in reality, the only safe place is in God's secret place, where hearts are exposed and covenant is restored and celebrated. The grass is not always greener on the other side. If you are lacking connection in your marriage, it may be an invitation to seek out the treasure that lies within. If you are too exhausted for the adventure of rediscovery, my prayer for you is that you are supernaturally recharged and reignited with passion for your spouse. Honestly, some of the deepest discoveries and rediscoveries are birthed in some of the most painful circumstances. Never give up. This is where faith is tested and proven to be effective. This is where we witness the power of covenant.

Chapter 15

Silencing the Language of Selfishness

"Dying to the old with the willingness to become one, is the ultimate act of marriage."
Traci

We live in a society that encourages focus on self. There is a healthy aspect of this, like self-care in health and well-being, which is very important. But there is a twisted aspect of self-focus that's unhealthy, causing us to disregard our impact on others. The healthy aspect moves us into building a better self so we can love others well. The unhealthy aspect would be "do what makes you happy no matter how it hurts someone else." That, of course, is total selfishness.

Selfishness is the enemy of a good marriage. Most everyone has an element of selfishness at one time or another, but the greatest freedom comes from letting go of self. I believe this is the type of surrender in which Jesus said, "You must be born again." We have created various philosophies and doctrines based on that phrase, but I think of it in the simplest terms. Consider the following.

Before birth, we breathe amniotic fluid, the life-sustaining substance of the womb that envelops us and protects us. We are fed and given life by the connection to our mothers' blood supply. Being born again places us in the "womb" of Heaven where we breathe in the liquid love of God. We become one with the Life-giver, Sustainer, Creator, and Nurturer of our souls. We thrive on our connection to His Spirit. The heartbeat of God feeds us, nourishes us, and grows us. When we learn to be in that place, we can step into the world and live and breathe, cord never cut. In Him we live and move and have our being. We can live the life we were created for, in communion with the One who first loved us.

Being born again requires the dying of the old (ways and identities), laying down our flesh and all that is attached to it, drowning willingly so that we may live. Birth can be violent, yet there is rest and peace, awe and wonder to be seen.

I believe this relates to marriage, in a sense. To lay down self and immerse ourself into the life of another, and allow them to immerse themselves into us, requires a rebirth. Dying to the old with the willingness to become one, is the ultimate act of marriage. It's a whole new world in which I have to look from outside of myself. Even before I breathe the words, "I love you," I must ask myself, "Have I been patient? Have I been kind? Have I envied? Have I paraded myself? Been puffed up? Have I behaved rudely? Have I sought my own way? Have I been easily provoked? Have I thought evil? Have I rejoiced in iniquity? Do I rejoice in truth? Do I bear all things, believe all things, hope all things and endure all things?"

> *Selfishness is the enemy of a good marriage.*

When we consider what the Scriptures say that love is, we have to then consider those questions. It is in those verses, that we discover

112

love is selfless. Christ put selflessness on display, yet we seem to struggle with laying down self. Does this have to do with fear? My son once said something profound that caused me to question my own fear:

Why do we fear love? Because we fear having to give something in return. If God is love and we are made in His image and likeness, would that not also make us Love? So then it must be true that to love another is to see the face of God. It must be true that when we are truly filled with love, our spirit must resonate in a wonderful way with His. So why can I not look at you and say, "You owe me nothing. You need to do nothing other than be yourself to deserve it. You do not have to do anything to maintain it. You do not have to fear it. It simply is something that is. And it is something that cannot be taken away. I love you?" One soul to another, one heart to another, why do we fear the love that comes from one another? For the same reason we fear the love that comes from God. We think it demands something of us. When truly, it demands nothing. Love's intent is to love. You are loved.

I appreciated his thoughts. Those are good questions. Can you look at your spouse and say:

"You owe me nothing."
"You need to do nothing other than be yourself to deserve my love."
"You do not have to do anything to maintain it. It's something that can't be taken away."

Would making those statements scare you? This kind of love requires the demolition of selfishness. Whether you believe yourself to be selfish or not, try the following exercises.

1. Make a conscious effort to become aware of how often you think of yourself.

2. Ask yourself if you make others' challenges and triumphs about yourself.

3. Practice a daily act of selfless giving.

4. Make a list of things that make your loved one happy.

5. Acknowledge people around you. Even in the grocery store, take a good look at those who are working and serving. Consider what they might be feeling and/or facing.

6. Look for opportunities to appreciate your spouse's difference of opinion.

7. Volunteer time and/or donate to those in need. (How can you meet your spouse's need?)

8. Practice empathy. Try to identify with your spouse's and others' feelings.

9. Admit when you're wrong. (It's really important to be able to acknowledge where you fall short).

10. If you're having trouble not focusing on self, ask the Holy Spirit to show you the moment when that began in your life.

11. Ask the Holy Spirit for the gift of the fruits of the Spirit in your life.

On the topic of silencing the language of selfishness, Bill has passed on some words of wisdom to our children that pertain to marriage and relationship in general:

"These are just a few of the things I want my kids to know. Some of these were passed down to me from my father. I didn't believe some of them when I was young, but now on this side of life, I've surrendered to the wisdom that all of these things were truer than I ever knew.

~ You're going to do some things well, and you're going to do some things badly. When you do well and get praised, give it to God. Don't let accolades make you complacent. Success is a combination of dreaming and work. One without the other will not serve you well.

~ When you hurt someone, own it and make it right. It's God that defines your eternity, and only He knows how forgiven you are. But it is your relationships with people that define the experience you have in this life.

~ You won't gravitate to those who love you the most, but to those who accept you the most. When you allow those who accept you to rise above those who truly love you, somebody is going to get hurt. It will only be the grace of the people you hurt and the people who love you that keeps your life from being defined by your lowest moments. People who love you will protect you if you hurt them. People who merely accept you will destroy you if you hurt them.

~ Surround yourself with people with whom you can be completely transparent and vulnerable. Choose those people wisely when you don't need them, because you're rarely thinking wisely when you do need them. But don't limit your counsel to your friends. Get a professional counselor in your life who has dismissed themselves from ever being a friend. That person may be the most honest person you ever speak with.

~ Rejection can be a brutal teacher. When people don't want to stand close to you, it's usually because you stepped in something. Selfishness is when you step in something on purpose and blame others for not accepting it. Selfishness is a rocket ride to a lonely life because when you step in something, people don't want you walking into their house.

~ Live a life filled with abundant experiences that you wouldn't mind telling your grandkids about. Judgment and grace are inevitable, but you only get to keep what you give away.

~ Everything, every moment, every breath, every heartbeat, will hinge on this question from Jesus Christ, "Who do you say that I am?" There is nothing more important than your answer to that question.

Chapter 16

Recovering From the Sickness of Secrecy

"The god of the ego demands far more sacrifices than anyone of us can offer."
Bill

The ego, or self, thrives in acceptance. The most bizarre fetishes and lifestyles find validation when people agree that they have merit and create a community around a way of being. People give consent and permission to lifestyles that others might find repulsive. Yet when someone is vulnerable and honest, at least you know what you're getting into. When actions that are not consensual start happening, things start going especially badly. It's not uncommon for people with deep personal passions or taboo perspectives to bury them beneath the collective acceptance of the Christian marriage covenant. When those issues of the heart start screaming for attention, the occasion for selfish fulfillment arises.

In doing research for this book I have talked with a couple who owns a popular fetish video hosting service as well as the owners of one of the most successful adult toy companies in the world. They revealed that there is literally not a single thing that you could think of that hasn't become a fetish in which people search for satisfaction or fulfillment. As an example of how wacky and weird things are, one of the most surprising and successful fetishes they revealed had nothing to do with nudity. It's called financial dominance and involves a young lady, fully clothed, who simply films herself yelling derogatory things aimed at rich men and ended in her demanding they send her money. And they would. Apparently there are powerful and wealthy men in the world whose existence is in being surrounded by people intimidated by their presence. So they are willing to pay a beautiful well dressed woman to tear them down and intimidate them into giving up their money, or their "power." This is just an example of the strange lengths people will go to in order to meet the needs of the ego or self. Now I'm aware that most people reading this book would shrug that off as someone who has issues that they can't relate to. But there are probably a couple of you who are thinking, "That's kind of hot. Yeah, I'm down." But I'm betting that, like most people with strange sexual appetites, you wouldn't want anyone to know. It's a secret! And here's the soil where big problems grow.

I remember sitting down with a man who dealt with a strong sexual addiction, yet he thought his wife didn't know and he wasn't about to tell her. He was sure she would never approve of the things he desired, especially since, though they included her, they involved people other than her. What he didn't realize is that she knew there was something hidden. Not wrong actions, just hidden thoughts. And here's an important point. Anything hidden from covenant is wrong. Secrecy and intimacy don't go together. So if killing intimacy in your marriage is the goal, introduce a secret lifestyle that you don't tell your spouse about. This man kept his secret from his spouse to "protect her." Yet this is foolishness, because even the most simple minded person can tell when something has gone wrong and division has happened between hearts that used to be united. To say yes to covenant is to surrender to union.

So why do people harbor secrets, especially when the keeping of a secret requires layers of lies? That shouldn't be too hard to understand. Lying is just one "self" exercising dominance over another by deception. Even when you're fooling someone for their benefit (like a surprise birthday party) there's an adrenaline rush. There's something about deception that makes the deceiver feel powerful. And this is why it's so destructive. That power becomes like a drug, because you have now taken control of a portion of a person's mind by inviting them to believe something that you know isn't true. Now you know something

> *Deception is a drug.*

they don't know and that's what gives the liar the power. When a couple goes through betrayal, one of the most difficult elements to understand is not what the offending spouse did, but the unraveling of the lies that the offended spouse has to deal with to catch up to the present reality. No matter what anyone says at this point, they struggle with feeling left behind, powerless, hopeless, and weakened. The pain of selfishness causes a virus to be released within the covenant. But the selfishness isn't satisfied. It's actually spreading. Now, even the offended spouse is selfish.

Who could blame them for being selfish? They were innocent. They were minding their own business, going about life as if things were fine, and then suddenly, the secret explodes onto the scene. You saw a text come through on their phone, walked by their computer with the email left open, overheard a late night phone call, saw credit card charges that didn't make sense, or heard it from a friend who heard it from a friend who…And now your life is dismantling. The destruction is painful and personal, and just as you felt like the center of their universe in love on your wedding day, now you feel like the center of their hatred and the object of their punishment.

"How could you do this to me?!?!?"

It's one of the most common phrases that the victimized self screams in these moments and it's been spoken into the atmosphere countless millions of times in every culture in every language. At this point, the betrayer, listening to their spouse scream in hurt and anger, is grasping at straws to find a way to make it stop. Seeing their spouse in pain, they suddenly have an awakening realization and that's that they never thought about their spouse in the middle of their selfishness. In a feeble attempt to try to fix the situation, the betrayer often blurts out one of the most revealing and foolish statements that could ever be uttered in this situation.

"I wasn't even thinking about you! It wasn't about you! You weren't even a thought!"

And there it is. Nothing is fixed by this statement. Now we have two, fully selfish people, in pain, wondering who they are and how they got here. Pay close attention to these next words, because though they are raw and brutal, they can bring you home. Self-centered ego shackled us the moment we looked away from the one we once loved with our whole heart, and I don't mean just your spouse. At some point, the ego draws your attention from your spouse, your children, and even from God. When we lose the perspective of the other-centered, self-giving love of the God who formed us, we wander in the dark from temporal fix to temporal fix, searching for our "self." What I'm about to say may be extreme and uncomfortable, but there's someone who needs to hear it: In searching for our "selves," we may even pay strangers to degrade
120

us. We might invite people and objects into every orifice on our human body, and when that isn't enough, we invite more people to get involved. To heighten the rush, perhaps we introduce substances into the mix and in a drug-induced haze, eventually wake up covered in every fluid the human body can produce. We might choose the motivation of money and power to feed the greed burning in our soul, and left unchecked, this empty existence becomes a game to win at the expense of everyone else. No amount of money, titles, trips, parties, partners, mergers, acquisitions, clothing, or jewelry can mask this new reality.

We have become our own god to be worshipped and given sacrifices. And the god of the ego demands far more sacrifices than anyone of us can offer. In all of this, we are losing the race to outrun the shame that has come to exist, that is, as long as we can feel. So we now work to kill our ability to feel. The very quest to feel as good as humanly possible ends with feeling so much pain that we now want all of the feeling to stop. In a lifetime of personal friendships with celebrities, political leaders, sports figures, preachers, and rock stars, I've seen that this journey to find your "self" is universal with varying degrees of intensity. The problems have just begun though, because we were not created to numb our emotions. We were created to find our life, breath, and satisfaction at rest in the affection of God and pure affection for one another.

1 Peter 4:8 says, *"Above all, love one another deeply, because love covers over a multitude of sins."* Grace and love is the only cure for the destruction left in the wake of a self-centered perspective.

The authentic self, the true you, and the character and nature of the God who made you is found in 1 Corinthians 13. Replace the word "love" with the revelation of God as an other-centered, self-giving, relationship of love known as Jesus. Family is what He's creating. It's what He's been creating all along,

> *There is no distance or separation between you and God right now.*

which is why we can know God as Father. The prodigal son parable reveals the Father's heart is to let your self take its journey without condemnation, and yet when you forget that you're His child, He never stops being our Father. Read this now with new eyes and see who He is, and in Him, see who you truly are.

1 Corinthians 13:4-8 *Christ* is patient, *Christ* is kind. *Christ* does not envy, *Christ* does not boast, *Christ* is not proud. *Christ* is not rude, *Christ* is not self-seeking, *Christ* is not easily angered, *Christ* keeps no account of wrongs. *Christ* takes no pleasure in evil, but rejoices in the truth. *Christ* bears all things, believes all things, hopes all things, endures all things. *Christ* never fails. In Christ, you have been made complete.

Go back and read this and see yourself in Christ. The only way to find this life is to surrender the old "self" to the cross, and to rise with Christ by faith with this revelation. There is no distance or separation between you and God now. Even that sin, and that sin consciousness, and all the people who betrayed you, and through all the people you have betrayed, the love of Christ remains. He remains to welcome you home, restored, reconciled, and free from all shame and guilt. This is the power of the blood of Jesus. His love covers us all.

Chapter 17

The Beauty of Four

"Your marriage is invited into being a living epistle that bears the greatest love story ever known, and it is a lasting story."
Traci

In our final chapter, we come back to the beginning to take another look at the four people you marry. Why four? It's quite interesting that there are four seasons, and the celebrations and feasts of the Bible are typically marked by seasons. On another note, there are the four elements: earth, wind, fire, and water. It is said that the number four relates to the creative ability of God. It is on the fourth day of creation that God created the sun, moon, and stars. Consider the four major cardinal directions: North, East, South, West. In the book of Ezekiel, there is mention of the "four wheels" and "four living creatures." The cherubim in this vision contained four faces. Jump to the New Testament and you'll find the four Gospels: Matthew, Mark, Luke, and John. The cross, where salvation was brought to all, and where we were reconciled to God, contains four points: left, right, top, and bottom. So what is the significance of four? Let's explore some parallels between these fun little facts and how they relate to marriage.

Seasons:

With each season, we experience beauty if we look for it. Whether spring, summer, fall, or winter, there is beauty to be found. When the heat is turned up in our relationships, when the cold freezes our hearts, the spring gives us hope, and the fall whispers, "There may be dark days ahead," we can still find beauty in the scenery and the warmth of promise. In the natural seasons of the earth, we don't believe we'll remain in that season, for we know there's another season ahead; change will come. But in the seasons of relationship, when hard times come, we almost always fail to see the promise and hope for days ahead. When difficulty arises, we wonder if there will be a tomorrow. *Will this marriage last? Did I make a wrong choice in a partner? Are we going to make it?*

Imagine with me that we aren't shaken by the person we think we are, or the person we think they are, or the person they seem to be right now, and instead, we recognize that we're going through a season that plays a role in who they (and who we) are becoming. Imagine that we don't freak out when trouble arises, and we have assurance that our foundation of love is sure to survive anything. The perspective you choose to have will either move you to a place of health or a place of falling apart before the opportunity to rebuild even begins. There may be long, hard winters ahead, but seasons change, the sun comes out and it's possible to fall in love with your spouse all over again.

Elements:

Earth - Earth is the third planet from the sun, and the only planet known to contain life. The majority of the planet is covered in water, a life-giving and sustaining source. Tectonic plates move below the surface. There's groaning, shifting, changing, and response to the forces of the planets around us. There is gravity that keeps us grounded. Miraculously, there is a indescribable balance of chemical elements that keeps us alive. Like earth, marriage must be fed by the life-giving, sustaining source of love in order to stand the tests of shifting and shaking. When we breathe in and exchange the breath of life, whether through intimacy or mere words, we ground each other in the midst of change, no matter the pressure and positioning of outside forces. When we keep ourselves aligned with our Maker, the elements mix to keep us thriving in abundant life.

Wind - So much can be said about wind. This powerful, unseen force whose beginnings and end are unknown; it both affects and empowers us in our daily lives. Isn't it amazing that something you cannot see with your eyes can make a huge impact? Whether it's moving like a gentle whisper or swirling like a hurricane, things of earth are moved. Humans have learned how to harness the wind for the benefit of mankind. In our marriages, whether it's a season of whispers and nudges or a time of raging storms, we can learn to navigate those winds, harness it for our good, and practice flowing with the wind of the Spirit. There, life is found. Where winds of destruction come, God makes it possible to clean up the debris and rebuild.

Fire - Fire, the chemical process of combustion. A source of light, heat, and power. Again, fire is a mixture of elements coming together with the ability to either bring life or destruction. It's a necessary part of life. In marriage, we can burn with passion that can either bring life or destruction. At times, we lack passion which indicates that the "smoldering wick" needs ignition. Perhaps you feel completely cold and hopeless, but you were made by the

125

"All-consuming Fire," and anything is possible with Him. It's interesting to think about God leading His people with a cloud by day and a fire by night. And it's also a beautiful comfort to know that He walked in the fire with Shadrach, Meschach, and Abednego, keeping them unscathed and without even the smell of smoke. In John's vision in the book of Revelation, he described seeing "something like a sea of glass mixed with fire," on which those who had been victorious over the beast stood, holding "harps of God." What beautiful imagery. No matter where you are in your marriage, God is there with you and there's promise of walking in victory.

> *There is mystery within your spouse whether you are aware of it or not.*

Water - We see water right away in Genesis 1:2. A formless void in darkness, God swept over and hovered over the face of the waters. Water, that very essential element to all life, and we are to be living springs of water, giving life to those around us. In the scriptures, we see that whether raging waters or peaceful waters, He is there. His word and His very breath bring peace and refreshing.

Every marriage contains moments that challenge us to keep our head above the waters. Instead of fighting the currents, that's where I've found the necessity to lie back and float, and allow the Father to carry me through times of difficulty. It's in those times when we feel like failures and disappointments that we have to make a conscious effort to remember we are actually sources of living water. No matter what element is touching our lives, whether positive or negative, our Father is always there. Christ in the midst of us, the hope of glory. When His voice seems lost in the elements, we must remember He is the Maker of those elements,

126

and nothing can separate us from His love. Press your heart into the One who chose the fourth day to create the sun, moon, and stars. He gives light and direction, so that you'll never be lost. He lights our path in the darkness, and if we just look for it, we can find the points of light. He is the Master of direction. The four cardinal points, the North, East, South, and West, and everything within them belongs to Him. The Creator has you covered no matter which of those "four people" you are experiencing, and no matter how far or which direction you have gone.

I think of Ezekiel's vision and the bizarre images of the "four wheels" and the "four living creatures," and how the mysteries of God lie within in covenants, even when we've completely lost sight of them. Like the children from C.S. Lewis' *The Lion, The Witch, and the Wardrobe*, if we don't actively move ourselves into another realm, we'll remain where we can only see the clothes hanging in the closet, and nothing more. There is mystery within your spouse whether they are aware of it or not. There is mystery within you, as well. Will you press through to see it? Will you think about the significance of the four Gospels and how they revealed to us the journey of God Himself upon the dust of the earth? The "Gospel" literally means "good story" or "good news." Matthew, Mark, Luke, and John had the privilege of recording an incomprehensible good story that shifted history and offered humanity an opportunity to live in alignment with our ultimate, true home. "In Him" we live and move and have our being. Now, your marriage and the "four people" that you experience are invited into being a living epistle that bears the greatest love story ever known, and it is a lasting story.

Love Story

"My eyes see perfection and there is no shame."
Traci

A suspended, undulating sphere
Trodden by guilty feet and fear.
Fractured ground, splintered souls
Desperate to uncover a pulse.

A suspended, undying Love
Our sins made Him a mourning dove.
Mending blood pours deep and wide
Sure to saturate His withering Bride.

Gently, He presses His ear to hear
Her chest rising and falling with fear.
"I am perfect Love. Open your lips and see.
Breathe, Bride. Exhaling you, inhaling Me."

His essence over her spirit glides
Penetrating until their hearts collide.
He reaches in and plucks hers out...
Giving His own. "She is Mine!" he shouts.

She shudders, eyes wide with rapture
Her chest rises, breathing deeply to capture,
Heaven's heartbeat now within her, eternally.

Intoxication, elation, joy and ecstasy.

"I have tasted. I have seen. What is this passion?
It lies deep within. It is You. And me You have fashioned.
Yet I cannot partake. Just look at me.
My garments, my clothes are tattered, You see?"

"Brilliant Bride, I am unaware of what you claim,
For My eyes see perfection and there is no shame.
I gave you my robe. You are pure and white as snow.
Every blemish, every stain, I no longer know."

She sighs, desperate to believe His words.
Afraid. She questions what she has just heard.
"It's impossible. Once a prostitute, my body marred,
No mercy could be so strong. Someday, You'll discard."

He dives into her soul with His spheres of grace,
Searching deeply within her, caressing her face.
"It is finished. See My hands, there you are engraved.
My blood has made you clean, no longer enslaved.

Suddenly, an explosion in her soul!
Nearly convinced that she is whole...
Tempted to shrink back and pull away,
But He firmly draws her to Him. "I am the Way."

"Open your lips. Breathe in deep.
My Bride. In My essence, you shall sleep.
You will dream, then awaken and see
All that you are is all of Me."

Daring to open herself and bare her soul,
She closes her eyes, her body falls into His hold.
A surge of life vanquishes every doubt.
Living waters flow. The curtain falls upon the drought.

A suspended, undulating sphere
Now carries the imprints of those that are dear.
Purchased, embraced in His grace.
Forever before Him, beholding His face.

About the Authors

Bill and Traci Vanderbush met at the age of five, and married at ages eighteen and nineteen. Together, they raised two beautiful human beings, Britain and Sara. Bill and Traci have served in various ministries, worked many jobs, owned a business, and experienced highs and lows which have fueled their passion to bring hope and empowerment to everyone they meet. They currently travel, speaking in conferences and churches around the world. Their consuming passion is to introduce people to the love and resurrection power of Jesus Christ, and to unveil the goodness of God, inviting people to walk in the truth of their identity.

For more information:
billvanderbush.com
tracivanderbush.com

Other Books and Resources by Bill
Purchase at billvanderbush.com

Reckless Grace Book (2020)
Grace is the ultimate expression of love.

We all know we need grace and forgiveness, but why is it so difficult to extend them to ourselves and others? In Reckless Grace, Bill Vanderbush and Brit Eaton challenge our understanding of forgiveness with powerful biblical evidence and show us how to step into the fullness of grace, bringing reconciliation and restoration to our relationships using:

-practical steps and accessible tools to help identify and overcome barriers to grace

-carefully crafted exercises and reflections that explore past and present hurts and work toward healing

-gentle guidance in becoming gospel-centered and releasing grace into a fallen world.

God isn't reckless, but the way he extends grace defies all reason. This inspirational book will help you learn to freely give what we have been freely gifted. Readers will learn how to escape the trappings of unforgiveness, embrace God's eternal grace, and be inspired to release grace over their lives and others.

Project 24 Download
Project 24 is 24 hours of teaching that will impact your perspective of your identity in Christ from a wide variety of angles. Upon purchase, you will be sent a link to a web page where you can stream or download all 24 hours of the audio and video files.

Messages Include:

Stewarding the Grace of God
Out of the Wilderness in the Power of the Spirit
You Are the Glory That Covers the Earth
Understanding the Mysteries of God
Being Love in the Darkness

Walking in Identity and Authority
Living Free From a Sin Conscious Mentality
The Vengeance of God
What Does God Believe About You?
Empowering Women in Ministry
Walking in the Ultimate Inheritance
…and many more.

Presence and Power Download

Presence and Power is 12 hours of teaching on walking in the supernatural life that Jesus Christ has given to you. This download also includes PDF files of notes for some of the messages. Upon purchase, you will be sent a link to a web page where you can stream or download all 12 hours of the audio and pdf files.

Messages Include:

Spiritual Joyfare
The Angelic Realm
Overcoming Demonic Influence
Living in the Presence
Being a Student of the Spirit
Greater Works Will You Do
Increasing in Favor
Words of Knowledge
Healing and Miracles
…and many more.

Quantum Preaching Masterclass

Quantum Preaching is 30-hour online public speaking Masterclass. What is Quantum Preaching? It is a supernatural quantity of anointing proportional in magnitude to the frequency of the revelation it represents. To simplify, it's the supernatural ability to connect with people where the revelation that's making your heart come alive becomes the revelation that makes their heart come alive.

The future belongs to the storyteller, and the power of story is the layers of revelation it contains. In this course you will learn to become a master storyteller no matter what age or background of the audience you are speaking to. Jesus said His words are Spirit and life, and when the Spirit of Christ lives within you, your words are far more than just sound. Life and death are in the power of the tongue. Do you know what you're releasing? If you have a longing to release life, this Masterclass is for you!

quantumpreaching.com

Other downloadable messages:

When Religion Comes Crashing Down
The New Covenant Reformation of the Church
Angels, Demons, and Spiritual Joyfare
Restoring Revelation
and much more!

Other Books by Traci

The Porches of Holly (2015)

In the midst of long-held secrets, extramarital affairs, and addictions, a supernatural force visits the small community of Holly and awakens hearts that were once threatened by destruction. The trials of life chose their victims at random. Lies knew no boundaries. And neither did the grace of God. An unseen presence pursued the resurrection of the dead and the sight of the blind. Local pastor, Dylan Vanberg, battles his own torment as he comes to realize the power of grace while the town newspaper reporter, Jackson Sawyer, begins to understand the power of words. The porches of Holly[?]where old stories are repeated, babies are rocked, and kisses are given. Where life happens. What secrets do these porches hold and what stories will they tell?

The Windows of Holly (2018)

After a supernatural force visited the tiny town of Holly to invade the affairs and long-held secrets of its residents, Dylan Vanberg found himself reeling over the return of his ex-wife, Lynette. Now, the couple faces the fallout of their choices. A mysterious stalker rattles Dylan's peace, driving him to investigate. Local newspaper reporter, Jackson Sawyer, stands by his friend as they navigate through bizarre circumstances. Will vengeance win or will redemption find its way into the hearts of accusers? The windows of Holly will reveal what truly lies within. Are you ready to see?

Study Guide for Discussion for the Modern Novel, The Porches of Holly (2020)

The Porches of Holly Study & Discussion Guide was created to be a companion for the novel, The Porches of Holly. The Study Guide can be used for individual study or group studies and/or book clubs. The guide was inspired by a book club who chose the novel as a focus for discussion and Scripture study. Various Scriptures are woven throughout the novel. Each individual participating in the study group or book club should have their own copy of The Porches of Holly Study & Discussion Guide. Dive in and explore the thoughts behind the characters of the town of Holly. Discover the hidden meanings of the characters' supernatural dreams and visions. Become acquainted with the Scriptures regarding grace, humility, the power of Christ's blood, and more as we walk through the story. It's a journey that will bring healing to the heart, mind, and soul, igniting hope in the reader.

Soul Reformation: Wholeness for the Body (2017)

Soul Reformation is a simple, short prayer and meditation project inspired by the author's personal experience as she sought relief from pain that was triggered by the memory of a traumatic car accident. Whether you are suffering from physical or emotional trauma, Traci's hope is that you will find some relief and encouragement as she shares her prayer and declaration for healing. Throughout the book, words of truth are intertwined with photographs of places where Traci felt the presence of God. She invites you to come to that place.

The Magic of our Forefathers: Awakening to the Value of the Older Generation (2014)

The Magic of Our Forefathers speaks of the hidden gifts of past generations and how they affect our lives and future generations. The author creatively unwraps the revelation of our ability to experience "time travel" through becoming aware of the value of our connection with the older generation. Through personal recollections and short stories, life lessons are revealed and hope-filled strength is given to the reader to overcome life's challenges. Basic principles regarding work ethic and walking through adversity are discussed as part of the journey.

Mr. Thomas and the Cottonwood Tree (2014)

After several recurring dreams about a tree where children would encounter God, Traci Vanderbush felt led to write a book for children that would release emotional healing, based on some of her personal experiences with the Father. Within the dreams, she kept hearing "Mr. Thomas and the Cottonwood Tree." She began researching cottonwoods and found that they exude a resin that some refer to as a "balm of Gilead." This confirmed to her that there would be healing within the story. Her husband, Bill Vanderbush, offered illustrations which they chose to keep simple and without color in order to allow children's' imaginations to paint a picture. Based in Austin, Texas, William and

Traci continue their journey into discovering the immense goodness and grace of God, and His ability to bring healing and redemption into the most impossible situations. As a wife and mother, Traci desires to inspire others to hold to a hope that exists beyond our realm.

Life with Lummox (2015)
Lummox is a cuddly, bubbly, bouncy, happy, lovable character that's full of fun and wonder. The hard part about being a Lummox is that the world is filled with stuff to trip on, knock over, and break. So to be a happy, hairy fellow means you smile with every smiley smile you've got. The story of Lummox encourages children to embrace and find treasure in the seemingly awkward and eccentric. Life with Lummox is written by Traci Vanderbush and delightfully illustrated by the love of her life, Bill Vanderbush. The rhythm and rhyme combined with jolly pictures will bring smiles and laughs to all who read. Perfect for reading to preschoolers. Early elementary students would also enjoy reading this delightful story. Adults of every age also find themselves smiling over Lummox.

Lummox and the Happy Christmas (2015)
The cuddly, bubbly, bouncy Lummox returns in this special Christmas adventure. Lummox encounters Santa and is given a gift that reveals the power of the baby boy who grew up to change the world. Join Lummox and his buddies as they celebrate the season. Beautifully illustrated by Bill Vanderbush. For children and adults of all ages!

Walking with a Shepherd (2006)
Is it possible that pastors fight depression? Is it possible that a large percentage of pastors' wives wish their husbands would consider another profession? On the outside, most churches look great, but on the inside, many churches are being ripped apart by gossip, division, and suspicions. Often, this leaves the minister's family wounded and struggling. In this book, you will discover some secrets of joy and learn simple principles of action and forgiveness. If you are a pastor's wife facing any of these issues, Traci Vanderbush has lovingly prepared a book of practical principles based on her own experience as a pastor's wife.

Freedom From Financial Shame (2019)

Are you suffering under the weight of financial shame? Do you feel hopeless as bills go unpaid? Are you working as hard as you can, but seem to be getting nowhere? Traci Vanderbush shares some of her and her husband's personal struggles: the weight of carrying a small business, finding an eviction notice on their door, backing out of their dream home one week prior to closing on it, job loss, and striving to meet the expectations of the American dream. Traci's stories are meant to lift up those who feel the shame of not being able to meet financial obligations, and infuse the reader with faith and hope to believe for the impossible.

A 12-Day Journey Into the Heart of Christmas (2020)

The year in which we believed clarity would come became the year that brought us things we never wanted to see: a global pandemic, clashes of racism, and escalated political upheaval. Christmas can be extra difficult for those who've suffered loss and are in isolation, so Traci Vanderbush was compelled to take readers into a 12-day journey of hopeful expectation of the One who came to save and redeem. Since Christmas is about celebrating the coming of Christ into a broken world, Traci decided to ask the question, "Jesus, what do You want for Christmas?" The answer led her to writing this nostalgic 12-day journey into the heart of Christ. Come and find warmth in the presence of the King

Tax-deductible giving is through Faith Mountain Ministries at:
vanderbushministries.com

Made in United States
North Haven, CT
16 November 2021